The Great Employee Handbook

Making Work
and
Life Better

Quint Studer

Published by:
Fire Starter Publishing
913 Gulf Breeze Parkway, Suite 6
Gulf Breeze, FL 32561
Phone: 850-934-1099
Fax: 850-934-1384
www.firestarterpublishing.com

ISBN: 978-0-9828503-3-6

Library of Congress Control Number: 2011945906

Printed in the United States of America

I wanted to be a productive worker. And in spurts I was. Notice the word *spurts*. The first step to being more productive in work and life was to make sure my own head was on straight. This journey began in December of 1982 when I turned my life and will over to the care of God as I understood him. I am grateful for the Grace of God and the Friends of Bill W.

The next blessing was my marriage to Rishy in 1984. Her steady belief in the journey and steady support of my taking the risk to leave a secure job for the unknown made possible what impact I have. Thank you, Rishy, for always being here for me.

I want to thank my father. From day one he demonstrated a great work ethic, having worked for General Motors for 41 years in a variety of roles. I am grateful to my mother for talking about her work as a nursery school teaching assistant each night at dinner. It left an impression on me

regarding the impact that a supervisor has on a person—
and not just at work. People take bosses home. Children
hear the conversations. The impact of a work environment stretches far beyond the workplace.

Of course, my appreciation also goes out to my five
wonderful children: Quin, Rebecca, Katye, Mallory, and
Michael. I have felt so much support from all of you.

Thank you to the many coworkers over the years who
tolerated my own growth as a worker and to those who
still have patience with me today.

Lastly, I want to thank the many of you who have taken
time to learn and to share what you've learned with me
and with others. We are all students of life. We are all
teachers.

My hope is that this book will be helpful to you in pre-
venting some situations that could prove painful, in rein-
forcing you are on the right track, and in helping you in
your work life and your outside of work life.

Thank you to the many organizations that do their best
to create great places for people to work. I have learned
that like there is no perfect person, there is no perfect
workplace. We are all on the same journey, and I am
grateful for the opportunity to be part of life.

TABLE OF CONTENTS

How to Use This Book

Welcome to *The Great Employee Handbook*. As the title indicates, it's written for employees—and because leaders are *also* employees, it's a helpful resource for all.

When an individual at any level is able to fully engage in their job and develop the sense of ownership and the skill set that make them valuable, they benefit in many ways. When leaders are able to help *all* employees achieve these goals, the whole organization benefits. It becomes unstoppable.

This book is meant to be an easy read with a big impact. Its chapters are short and to the point and filled with "how-to" tips the reader can put into practice right away. Each chapter begins with the *why*, as I've found that when you can help people understand the benefit of making a change they are far more willing to do so (and far more invested in the results) than they would be otherwise.

Here are a few ways to use *The Great Employee Handbook*:

If You're an Employee:

- If you're just entering the workforce, read the book cover to cover. While it's written as a reference guide and isn't meant to tell a consecutive story, it's an overview of challenges you're likely to encounter in your work with bosses, coworkers, and customers. Every chapter includes insights and best practices that can take an entire career's worth of experience to learn.

- Read it when you're starting a new job. It will help you get off on the right foot with the boss and coworkers.

- If you have been on the job awhile, read it. When a situation comes up that you're not sure how to handle, refer to the appropriate chapter. The book is packed with tips proven to solve common problems and get results.

- If your role in the organization changes, zero in on the chapters that will help you gain or polish needed new skills.

- If you're seeking to advance inside your company, read (or re-read) the book. It will help you brush up on the skills that make people high performers.

- Give a copy to a high school or college student or someone you know who is starting their first job (or a new job).

If You Supervise Others:

- Share it with all employees "just because." It's a great refresher course for most people. It most likely reinforces what you're already trying to teach and model.

- Give copies to employees who are training for supervisory roles. It's important that they live the values they want others to model. The book will serve as a reminder of what it means to be a great employee.

- Hand out copies of the book as a welcoming gift and training tool for new employees. It's a good way to say, "This is what is expected."

- Share it with employees when you're seeking to implement a culture change or move an initiative through. It's the perfect way to remind individuals what it means to take ownership and to be fully engaged.

- Use it as an educational/motivational tool for those who are struggling. You might want to give out copies of the book at performance reviews.

- Read it yourself to improve your own performance. Many of the topics are universal and apply to people at all levels. Anyone from frontline customer service people to CEOs can benefit from learning about time management, how best to handle gossip, how to build emotional bank accounts with others, and so forth.

I hope you will find this book helpful. I enjoyed writing it. I hope you will enjoy reading it...and will see the positive results unfold in your life and in your organization for many years to come.

Quint Studer

INTRODUCTION

M ost of us want to do a great job. I really believe that. But often I find we get into situations we just don't know how to handle. After all, there aren't many formal training programs that teach people how to figure out what matters most to a boss (and deliver on it), or how to manage competing projects that both have tight deadlines, or how to respond to a gossipy coworker.

The answers to problems like these usually come from experience. It really *is* the best teacher. There is a magical time many people naturally reach when our emotional maturity, intellectual capacity, and work experience come together and allow us to handle situations that previously would have baffled us. The goal of this book is to help readers get to that point earlier. It's the book I wish was around in my own career.

My father retired from General Motors at the age of 60, after 41 years on the job. If I had talked to him back then I think he could probably have solved many of the problems I talk about in this book. But who wants to wait until they're ready to retire to know how to be happy and successful at work? And who can afford to?

Today we don't have the luxury of a lot of time to figure out how to get it right. New employees, for instance, have to hit the ground running and show value right away. (Long onboarding (orientation) processes and learning curves are as much a thing of the past as working for the same company all your life and retiring with a gold watch.)

And then, once we become experienced employees, we have to keep showing our value every day. It's a reality that comes with working in a rapid-fire business world in an unforgiving economy.

I'm not saying the new way is bad. Actually, it's energizing and deeply rewarding. But it does require far more of an "ownership" mindset than the old way did. Fortunately, there is a lot individuals can do to change their workplace for the better—if only someone gives them the tools that are proven to work.

I have been fortunate enough to work with thousands of employees at various levels inside many organizations. I have observed all sorts of challenges employees must deal with on a day-to-day basis. I've seen what works and what doesn't. I've been mentally collecting all of this knowledge for years and I finally decided to turn it into a book.

The Great Employee Handbook is meant to help readers achieve their own potential, to become happier and more successful at work, and to positively impact the lives of those around them. And though I am best known for my work in healthcare, this book is written for people in all industries, in all kinds of organizations, and at all levels.

I hope it will provide a good foundation for helping new employees "onboard" quickly and will also help seasoned professionals think about issues they may be struggling with from a new perspective.

You'll see there are chapters on working best with the boss, with coworkers, and with customers. Chapters have been kept short. (I know I'm often too busy to read big, thick chunks of information and I suspect you are, too.) Also, I've tried to explain the *why* upfront every time. I find that when people understand why they're being asked to do things in a different way—when they understand why it works and that it *does* get results—they are far more willing to make the change. In fact, they *want* to.

If there's one overarching lesson that applies to every tip in the book, it's simply this: We can't change or control other people, but we can change and control ourselves. Leaders have always asked me "How can I fix this department?" or "How can I fix this person?" The answer is sometimes we can't.

But I find that when I stop focusing on fixing others and start working on myself, sometimes the others change for the better right along with me. (Positivity spreads just like negativity.) And we as individuals always become much happier and more successful when we focus on ourselves. (The maturity of a person and even an organization can be measured by how much time they spend fixing themselves rather than worrying about fixing others.)

I've also learned that when people take responsibility for their own happiness and success, opportunities open up. There was a time in my career when I tried to escape from an unhappy situation by finding a new job. I applied for a lot of positions and went on a lot of interviews. But I think interviewers sensed I was unhappy and did not want to hire an unhappy person.

So I made a decision: Due to my unsuccessful exit plan, I would spend the next year working really hard on doing the best job I could do. Just throwing my heart into my work made me a happier employee. (It also made the people around me happier.) Lo and behold, I ended up getting the next job I interviewed for. It was a job I really wanted, and years later, after several career milestones had been achieved, it led to my starting my own company.

When one works hard to maximize their own potential—to be the very best employee they can be—they'll find themselves a lot happier on the job. That's really what this book is all about. There is no utopia or happily ever after—there are bad days in every workplace—but overall you can be fairly happy where you work most of the time.

I'm a firm believer that when we're happy with where we work, we're happy when we leave work. When we're happy when we leave work, then we make better spouses, parents, friends, and members of society. That means not only do we improve the quality of life for ourselves, we also improve the quality of life for our families and the community. Not bad for a day's work!

Quint Studer

SECTION ONE:

WORKING BEST WITH YOUR BOSS

Chapter One:

Put Your Best Foot Forward in the First 90 Days

T he first 90 days at a new job can be filled with stress and anxiety. In an attempt to avoid stepping on anyone's toes, getting on the wrong side of a new co-worker, or making a mistake, it's often tempting to just keep your head down and lay low. But to do that is to miss a big opportunity—often, these first three months are the perfect time to really catapult yourself forward at the company.

Today business moves at lightning speed. The minute you start with a company it's time to start finding ways to show your value. Your first months are crucial because during that time the boss and your coworkers will be forming their first impressions of you.

When you hit the ground running, you can immediately start living up to the reason that the boss hired you. High-performing coworkers will see that you may be a fellow high performer, and they'll be much more willing to invest time training you and teaching you the ways of he company. If they don't see that potential in you they might think, *Oh, they're not going to provide the relief I need quickly enough*—and move on to mentoring someone else.

I say all of this not to make you even more anxious when you start a new job, but to encourage you to be a results-focused high performer right from the get-go. Your first 90 days will set the temperature for the rest of your time with that company so it's important to make them count.

Here are a few tips to help you make those first 90 days really count:

Make a great first impression. Yes, it's absolutely important to do your best work, but use those first 90 days to make a great first impression in the traditional sense as well. Follow the company's behavior standards and dress code to the letter. Be on time. Meet every deadline and deliver ahead of schedule if you can. Double-check all e-mails and other communication for correct spelling and grammar. Learn all of your coworkers' names and positions. Keep your office or workspace clean. In other words, start your new job by being a great citizen for the rest of your coworkers. They'll instantly appreciate your good manners and your results-driven attitude.

Set goals and milestones for yourself early on. Express to your boss that you really want to hit the ground running. Work with them to set realistic goals for your first 90 days. Ask if it would be possible to have a progress meeting every 30 days so that you can address where you are with your goals and also receive feedback on what's working and what isn't. This is a great way to show the boss that you want to be a productive member of the staff, and it's also a great opportunity to start building a strong relationship with them.

Learn what the company brand is all about. During your first 90 days, read, observe, ask. Do whatever you can to learn about the company's philosophy and how it could affect the way you do your job. The company where you last worked might have been all about price and making sure customers knew it had the lowest prices around. But maybe this new company is first and foremost about providing great service. When you have a strong understanding of the company's brand, you can better chart out what you can do to add value to it and to keep the company moving toward its goals.

Embrace company values and standards. Follow the "rules," both written (in the employee handbook and official standards of behavior documents) and unwritten. It demonstrates your investment in your new job and demonstrates respect for leaders and coworkers.

Be positive. If you are stressed, nervous, or anxious about your new position, understand it's normal. Instead focus on what you're excited about—being part of a great company, getting to know new coworkers, delivering great service to customers, etc. Be pleasant and courteous to others. Saying "Good morning" and "Have a good night" to the boss and your coworkers can really go a long way. It shows people you are likeable, and likeable people get more help and more training because others want to be around them. Keep negativity at bay. Don't complain about company policies, customers, or any coworkers. Put positivity out there and your coworkers will give it right back to you.

Don't become part of the gossip mill. It can be all too tempting to join in on workplace gossip, especially when you are the new guy or gal. After all, these interactions can make you feel like you're part of the group, but they're really no place for a new employee. You do not want to be associated with gossip in the workplace. It is negative communication that can easily lead to trouble, and it makes those involved seem untrustworthy. Instead, focus your energy on building positive, work-based relationships with coworkers.

Excuse yourself when rumors become the topic of discussion and gently remind coworkers that passing on rumors could damage their own reputations. If the gossip is company-related, consider approaching the boss to let them know that rumors are floating around and that explanations would be greatly appreciated by all employees.

Learn your boss's and coworkers' *whats*. Everyone has a *what*. It's that certain something that needs to happen in order to be satisfied. The boss's *what* might be relentlessly meeting deadlines or showing up on time. For the coworker in the cubicle next to you it might be a tidy and organized workspace. The first 90 days are a great time for you to carefully observe those around you to find out what their *whats* are. And if you can't figure it out, ask! When you can deliver on their *whats*, your coworkers and the boss will think very highly of you.

Familiarize yourself with customer preferences. In addition to learning the boss's and your coworkers' *whats*, pay close attention to your customers' preferences. Make note of who the business's "regulars" are. Keep cards on each customer you work with and jot down what they like and dislike, how they prefer to be communicated with, and any other information they may provide about their work or professional life. Use everything you compile to provide them with great customer service every time you see them.

Follow up frequently. As you take on your first tasks or projects, stay in front of the boss. Make sure they know what you are working on and be upfront about your progress. If you run into a problem, let the boss know about it. They have a lot on their plate and won't want to feel they have to hold your hand through every task. When you follow up and let the boss know what you're working on, it eases anxiety and provides them with the opportunity to guide you and make sure you are on the right track.

Maximize the experience you bring to the table. When you feel like you know the lay of the land and fully understand the company brand and goals, speak with the boss about any recommendations you might have. Maybe at your previous company orders were processed in a way that is more efficient than the way your new company does it. Maybe you know that a former coworker shares the new company's philosophy and work ethic and would fit right in. Or maybe you know of a vendor who provides great service and at a lower rate than the business your new company uses. When you've set a good foundation and have shown that you are a high performer who does great work, the boss will value your input and will appreciate your effort to find ways to make the company even better.

Ask questions. Remember, everyone at your new job had a first 90 days of their own. They know what it feels like trying to get the lay of the land at a new company. That said, don't be afraid to ask questions when you need guidance on a particular task or simply don't understand a particular instruction. Taking an extra second to ask for a clarification is much better than risking the possibility that a significant amount of time will have to be taken to fix a mistake. Asking questions is also a great way to start building a rapport with coworkers.

Be open to feedback. When you receive feedback from the boss or a coworker, don't take it as hurtful; take it as helpful. Learn to process it as the constructive feedback it is meant to be. Listen carefully to what they say and use that time to ask for any clarification that is needed. When you've had a chance to put their advice into practice, follow up with them to make sure you are meeting their expectations. Sometimes employees have a cavalier attitude and kind of "blow off" criticism. Great employees know that criticism is meant to help them do better work and grow professionally. They use it to their advantage.

Be a team player. You are not a one-person show. In order to set the right tone at the new job, be a productive member of the team. Give credit to others when they've done a great job. And when you're complimented on something, use the opportunity to manage up some-one you work with. When you show that you are a team player, people will want to work with you. You'll be able to get involved with higher profile projects and tasks, which will help you become more valued in the company.

Try to be problem-free. Don't draw unwanted or negative attention to yourself during your first months. During your first 90 days, avoid asking for any vacation days unless discussed prior to taking the job. If at all possible, don't take any sick days or leave work early because of appointments. Be as steady and consistent as possible.

Learn from the organization's high perform-ers. Keep an eye out for those coworkers who consistently reach goals, meet deadlines, and receive great feedback from customers. Mirror their best practices. If you run into problems during your first months, ask the high performers how they would handle the situations. And if you have a particularly good rapport with one high performer, don't be too shy to ask that person to be your mentor. Having a mentor is a great way to learn more about the company and the way it does business and to get feedback on your performance.

The first 90 days are your chance to make a positive impression on your boss and coworkers. Don't try to fly under the radar. Use this important time to begin to make your mark with your new employer. When others see what you're capable of, they'll be excited about working with you, and long-term productive relationships will begin to form.

CHAPTER TWO:

EXECUTE WELL

"Action is the real measure of intelligence."
—Napoleon Hill

E xecution has always been a challenge for companies. As workplaces get more and more complicated, it's harder to execute than it's ever been. And in a tough economy, it's an issue that can mean the difference between survival and failure.

As companies streamline their operations and look for ways to get more efficient, being known as a person who gets things done will serve you well.

So how well do *you* execute? Do you take quick, decisive, meaningful action day after day? Or do you often find yourself waiting on someone to give you your next assignment, redoing your work, or missing important deadlines?

If you seem to have trouble executing, there could be many possible reasons. For instance, maybe a coworker won't get you the information you need. Or you're a perfectionist who can't stop "improving" your work and just get it done already. Or your to-do list is too long. Or when

...e project gets to you there isn't enough time left to do your part.

These issues exist inside organizations. But great employees don't let them become excuses. After all, whether you save lives or sell cars or build websites or cater parties, your job is to do your job. To execute. That means coming to work on time and ready to take action. That means meeting deadlines and being a team player. That means really "owning" the job and doing what's necessary to overcome the obstacles.

It's true that in the past employees got a lot more guidance. But in a fast-moving, ever-changing global economy, most leaders don't have a lot of time to nurture people and monitor their work every step of the way. And that's why people who can work independently are so valued.

When you are a skilled "executer" you play a vital role in moving your company forward. You make life easier for leaders and everyone else. Rather than being a bottleneck, you're a facilitator. You're the rocket fuel that keeps the company moving ahead of the competition.

Here are a few tips to help you become a great executer:

Do the important things first. Often I find we let small, urgent tasks eat up the entire day. When 5:00 rolls around, we've barely started on the items that really matter. Don't let this happen. For example, rather than spend your entire morning answering all of your flagged e-mails, respond to only those that are emergencies, so that you can get started on the big items at the top of your to-do list. By tackling what matters most first thing and making good headway on critical tasks every day, you'll be less likely to find yourself in a desperate situation as the deadline approaches.

Keep your to-do list in front of the boss. In an economy where things change quickly, companies frequently have to take a step back and recalibrate. Something that was critical last week may have dropped to second or third place this week. That means it's a good idea to be proactive about making sure the boss knows what you're working on.

Don't assume that they'll let you know when it's time to change gears. Situations change and sometimes the boss doesn't have time to brief you. Maybe what you're doing is now obsolete, and the boss simply doesn't remember giving you the task.

When you show your to-do list to the boss, be sure to prioritize your tasks using an A-B-C method, with "A" tasks being the most important and "C" the least important. That way they easily see what your emergencies are and/or can help you reprioritize if necessary. If you're not in a position where you feel comfortable prioritizing your own list, ask the boss to do so for you. You might say, "I think Item 1 is the most urgent, but please let me know if I should move another task in front of it." It's *your* responsibility to ensure that you're working on the right things at the right time—and prioritizing and frequent reminders are the best way to make that happen.

Make sure you really understand the project. Sometimes at the start of a project people are not clear on what the outcome needs to be or what their role actually is in making it happen. As a result they may feel uneasy so they procrastinate. Or maybe they go down the wrong path and end up having to rework. Either way, lack of clarity is a major enemy of good execution.

The remedy is simple: Ask questions until you're sure you understand. Don't just clarify what your role is; ask about the *why*. Once you know the thinking behind the assignment, you'll not only be more likely to buy into it, you'll be able to ask intelligent questions and make the right adjustments. Good execution isn't just following orders and going through the motions; it's getting to the outcome in the best possible way.

Think it through upfront. What is the shortest distance from A to B? If you figure out the most efficient path from the beginning you'll greatly speed up the process. (Otherwise you might end up zigzagging through C, D, E, and F before you ever get to B!) Don't assume that just because something has "always been done this way" that it's the best way. Maybe things have changed inside the company or in the external environment that make the old way obsolete.

Thinking the project through early on allows you to do a better job of anticipating potential problems, setting deadlines, and planning your tasks. If you know that you are going to be out the week before a finished project is due, you'll know to: a) set an earlier deadline for yourself so that you get your portion done before you leave, b) make sure the project point person knows your schedule, and c) ask for items that you know you'll need ahead of time. In other words, even if you aren't quite ready for the data your coworker Jim is gathering, ask him for it now or let him know when you'll need it so that he will get it to you on time and everything can keep moving smoothly. This will keep you from making a lot of frantic last-minute requests—requests that derail other people's (equally important) work.

Remember, most projects are organic, not linear. Very rarely will you move sequentially from Step 1 to Step 2 to Step 3 and so on. Most likely, you'll be working in tandem with a team where each individual is working on a portion of the project. Be sure you're never the hold up. Keep your team leader and coworkers informed about what you're working on and when.

Keep it simple. Don't go through unnecessary steps or get people involved who don't really need to be. Make sure you know who your point person is, whether it's the boss or a coworker who is heading up a certain project. Run your questions through that person and that person only. Don't complicate things by asking coworkers questions they might not have the answers to or that might confuse them and what they're working on. Think carefully about who you need feedback from before you ask. Too many cooks in the kitchen rarely results in a delicious meal!

Assume the ball is always in your court. When you're assigned a task, do what you need to do to move it forward quickly. Don't ever let yourself be the holdup.

Sometimes, you may encounter a true roadblock that stalls your progress. If this happens and you can't solve the problem, go to the boss immediately and let them know what's going on. They may have a quick solution. But even if they don't, they'll know you are doing your part to keep the project moving. The idea is to tell the boss about it before they have to ask.

Don't let a few missing details hold a project hostage. Sometimes people may assume they need to have every last bit of information in order to get started on a project. This is not always true. (And if we're perfectly honest, many of us would have to admit it's a form of procrastination!)

It's often possible to complete big chunks of the project without the missing information. Make it a point to do as much as you can as early as you can without compromising the overall quality. (On the other hand, you don't want to do so much guessing that you end up going miles in the wrong direction!)

Finally, set deadlines with coworkers for when you need certain information and send persistent reminders. Depending on the situation, you might even let them know they are holding up the project. Don't assume they know.

Kick the procrastination habit. Volumes have been written on procrastination. It's true: There are many theories about why people put things—*important things*—off. In my mind, knowing why we procrastinate isn't nearly as critical as resolving to overcome the habit. Procrastination is a true enemy of good execution.

I have noticed this: When people really focus on completing a tough task instead of coming up with a million reasons not to, they quickly realize the payoff of "just doing it" far outweighs the momentary relief that comes from avoiding the painful task.

Do everything you can to make sure you deliver on time. Yes, there are times when deadlines cannot be met, but make it your goal to be sure such times are few and far between. One missed deadline leads to another and another and another. Before you know it, you'll have a difficult-to-improve reputation for being unreliable.

That said, if you need to work through the occasional lunch or stay late once in a while to meet a deadline, it's okay (as long as you have the boss's permission to do so!). Putting in those few extra hours is well worth missing out on the headaches they'll save later.

Don't let perfection be the enemy of execution. Many people work and work on a project and never seem to feel it's good enough to deliver. In an effort to "get it perfect" they miss deadlines, lose sight of the big picture, and, ironically, undermine their own success inside a company. The time and energy they spend obsessing over every last detail is almost always better spent on moving on to other tasks.

The truth is, in many cases 90 percent is good enough and 100 percent is overkill. No one is going to notice the last 10 percent of effort—and it's often that 10 percent that makes the project late enough to irritate the boss (or worse, the customer).

I've heard it said that life rewards action. I believe it. People who are more geared toward "getting it done" than toward analysis paralysis and perfectionism are always the most successful people. And a whole organization full of them is unstoppable.

CHAPTER THREE:

WHAT TO DO IF YOU FEEL THE BOSS IS THE PROBLEM

O ne of the most frequently asked questions I receive—the one that's at the top of everyone's list—is: What can I do if my boss is a low performer?

This chapter is near the front of the book because it centers on one of the most difficult issues an employee can face. It's tough enough to confront someone who we supervise about job performance issues and even tougher to have that difficult conversation with a peer—but taking on the boss may seem impossible. It may even seem career threatening.

Yet, if you're working for a boss you feel is the problem, you likely feel disillusioned and discouraged. Plus, you aren't being mentored and developed in the ways you desire. As a result, you pay the price. Other coworkers in your department struggle, too. The organization may not achieve its goals. And yes, even the boss loses out.

It's not easy to confront a low-performing boss—but it is possible. By taking assertive action, you may be able to help them improve their performance. This will benefit you and other team members in numerous ways. Ultimately, the boss may come to be grateful that you spoke up. I've seen many work relationships grow deeper and stronger when one party demonstrates the courage and honesty it takes to provide this type of feedback.

After talking with hundreds of staff and leaders who want to push through this barrier, I have some suggestions on what you can do if you feel your boss is a low performer. Try these:

Take a look at yourself first. Hold up the mirror. Ask yourself if you're really being fair. Is the boss a low performer or just falling short of perfection? Or are you comparing them to another boss with whom you had a closer working relationship? You have to fairly assess the boss's behavior without comparing them to your idea of a perfect boss or a leader you have great memories about.

Then, think about your own behavior. Make sure you are doing all you can to help your department, store, team, and so forth to achieve the desired results. Bosses appreciate someone who provides solutions. Find ways to take things off your boss's desk rather than piling new things on by pointing out problems with no solutions or ownership.

While the boss may not perform the way you wish, you will have a much better discussion about these issues if you are performing well yourself. Reaching out to your employee assistance program is also a good way to make sure other issues are not clouding your perception of the situation.

Think about the boss's to-do list. Even if you work really closely with your boss, they may be involved in projects that you're not aware of. You can be sure their plate is overflowing with tasks to complete, too. If they don't quickly get back to you on a certain project, it might not be because they are not concerned, but because they were hard at work on other tasks. Observe the boss, and if it seems they are indeed overworked, ask if there is any way you can help to lighten the load.

Look for progress over perfection. There are times when perfection should absolutely be expected (e.g., before an airplane takes off, before a medication is given, before a bill is sent out, or before a product is delivered). But the workplace consists of humans working with other humans, and none of us are perfect.

We all want the perfect boss and the perfect place to work, but the reality is we're never going to get it. I've visited companies that have won the Best Place to Work distinction and the Malcolm Baldrige Award, and even those organizations aren't perfect. What's even more important is that they know they'll never be. Instead, they focus on constant improvement and on being the best performers they can be.

If you're constantly thinking to yourself, *I wish the boss would stop using this or that phrase* or *I wish they would be as organized as the last boss,* you'll be constantly disappointed. But when you change your focus from wanting perfection to celebrating progress, you'll begin to see how hard everyone is working, including and especially the boss, and I think you'll start to enjoy your job a lot more.

Start with identifying what the boss does that you feel is helpful. Ask yourself: *Does the boss do many things well and a few things poorly?* It's easy for a few frustrating behaviors to cloud our judgment and overall view of our boss, in spite of some redeeming qualities. Let the boss know what is working for you first. Remember, recognized behavior gets repeated.

Here is an example: "Larry, I appreciate the time you spent with me this morning going over my to-do list. Your time on this very much helps me prioritize next steps, move more quickly, and achieve outcomes." By telling Larry that you appreciate his time and why, it becomes much more likely that Larry will make time for you next time you ask.

Another example: "Larry, I do appreciate your candid feedback on my performance and suggestions for improving my customer satisfaction scores. I'm grateful that you're willing to invest in my professional development by pointing out what I can improve on." (Here, you've let Larry know you can take candid feedback.)

Confront the problem. If you've already looked in the mirror, believe your own performance is consistently strong, and have shown maturity by welcoming potentially negative feedback, you're ready to take the next step with the boss who is still not meeting your expectations. I recommend using a "support-confront-support" technique. Basically, you combine what is working well with what is not. Be sure to emphasize that this is your perception of things. This will help the boss to be a more receptive listener who is less defensive.

Example: "Larry, I want to thank you for sharing the customer feedback cards with me. Your suggestion that I focus on making better connections with customers and the implementation tips you offered are really helpful to me. I've already noticed a lot of improvement. In fact, I think your tips helped me close two sales with customers who previously seemed reluctant to commit."

As you move on to the "confront" part of the conversation you might consider using impact messages to carefully communicate your feelings. This method will feel less accusatory to the boss. Here is an example:

"You know, this is just my own perception—you may not even realize it—but you just asked me a question and before I had finished answering, you started asking me another question. The impact is that we can't sufficiently address the problem or concern. What would help is if you made a note of your additional questions and then presented them to me over time. I think it would help us both keep from becoming overwhelmed and make the most of our time together. As I said, I do very much appreciate the investment you're making in me. It's clear your suggestions are helping me to meet my sales goals."

Typically, the boss will respond well to this kind of approach. The key is to start and end with the positives. Always use the words "It's my perception" when you have this kind of discussion. Also, try not to judge the boss too harshly. In my experience, most of the time, they are not aware of the full impact of their actions on you. This is because all too often, we don't take ownership for having these direct conversations. Instead we vent our frustrations with others who can't really help us.

Move to the DESK approach. Okay, so you've tried the tips above and haven't gotten anywhere. What's next? Meet with the boss using the Describe—Evaluate—Show—Know approach. Here's how it works:

D—Describe what has been observed. "Larry," you say, "thank you for your time. I would like to share my perception with you about the meeting yesterday. Please listen until I finish what I have to say. Yesterday at the sales meeting, you asked me a question, but did not allow me to complete my answer before you said, 'Sounds like we don't know what to do.'"

E—Evaluate how you feel. Evaluate how you feel or how your organization's policy, standard, or value is not being lived by your boss's behavior. "Larry, when this happened, I was hurt and embarrassed. I also believe that making that comment and interrupting me mid-sentence is not consistent with our organizational standards regarding respect."

S—Show what needs to be done. "My goal is to do well here, so I want you to know I can accept negative feedback if it is offered in a professional manner. Since I know we both want to achieve the same goals, I'd like to describe the best way to provide feedback to me. If you have concerns about what I'm saying, for example, just speak to me privately after the meeting and we can address them together then."

K—Know the consequences. You might sa, "Larry, if we cannot work out a way to communicate in a more productive manner, (then lay out what you are willing to do)." For example, you might suggest that you will need to bring up the issue with the boss's boss. Or if the situation is dire enough, you might suggest that the business is not the right place for you to work right now, even though it saddens you to say it. (Remember, you don't have to follow through on quitting, but perhaps you have signaled the importance of resolving this issue. However, if you go this route, you must be prepared for the consequences and how they might negatively affect you.)

I understand that using the DESK approach is not easy. It takes a lot of courage and persistence. However, I urge you to be brave. Working for someone who drains your energy will impact your health, create issues with coworkers, compromise your personal values and high standards, and eventually impact those you love when you take your frustrations home day after day.

Be prepared for potential reactions. Of course, the biggest reason we don't confront low-performing bosses is because we're afraid of how they might react. We picture the boss flying off the handle and firing us right there on the spot. You absolutely should prepare yourself for possible negative reactions. Depending on the boss's communication style, they may immediately recognize that what you've said is true and promise to improve in that area. On the other hand, they might become offended or upset. If this happens it's important for you to stay as calm as possible while also standing your ground. You might stress the positives once again and hen reiterate that if you could both improve in the ways discussed in the meeting the whole company would benefit.

Get support when you need it. It's also true that some behavior crosses the line when it's abusive, harassment, or too volatile to handle alone. In those cases, do reach out to the system your organization has in place and report such actions. Remember to access your company's employee assistance program. They can help you make sure that your perception is accurate and also provide key tips for managing the problem during this stressful time.

My experience is that being a supervisor isn't easy. I just don't think leaders come to work with hopes of ticking off a few employees and creating conflict. That said, there's a good chance that the boss will be receptive and appreciative of the honest feedback you offer when you address concerns directly. Typically, your working relationship will improve.

By taking the lead in resolving conflicts, you demonstrate healthy adult behavior to yourself, the boss, and the organization. It's not easy, but that's often true of doing the right thing. If, in the unlikely event that the above tips do not create the right environment, remember that in the long run you will be happier and more successful in a place with a better fit.

CHAPTER FOUR:

WHEN YOU BRING A PROBLEM, BRING A SOLUTION

D o you consider the boss the organization's official "problem solver"? Many employees do. When things aren't going well, what is your first impulse? Do you immediately drop the problem in the manager's lap? Or do you try to figure out your own solution?

I hope you do the latter, and there are several reasons why:

Reason #1: Like you (and almost everyone), the boss is really busy. Maybe they're even overwhelmed. The more you can help the boss keep their to-do list manageable, the more effective they'll be overall. Plus, they'll appreciate your willingness to take the initiative and to think creatively.

Reason #2: You are closer to the problem than the boss is. You've probably been thinking about it for a long time. Therefore, it stands to reason that you can come up with a better solution than they can—or at least a good "starting point" for a solution.

Reason #3: You're truly showing ownership of your area of responsibility. This contributes to a more entrepreneurial culture—which in turn creates a stronger, more innovative, more resilient company.

I've spent a lot of time talking with Studer Group® clients and other groups about this last point. Generally when I talk about what I have heard described as Park Ranger Leadership, I'm referring to the mindset taken by employees that "the bosses will figure it out." But the same principle applies at all levels.

What is Park Ranger Leadership? Basically, it's the attitude that "someone up there" will come to the rescue and lead you out of the (metaphorical) wilderness. People naturally tend to look to higher-ups for solutions, and it's understandable: Chances are, those higher-ups have always come through in the past.

But consider this: How great would it be if everyone at every level of authority figured out their own solutions? The solutions would be more practical and workable, the managers above them would be able to spend more time doing their jobs more efficiently, and so on and so on, all the way up to the senior level. Once everyone got into the habit of solving problems, it would start a chain reaction of innovation that could transform the future of the organization.

Most human beings have wellsprings of potential inside them. I really believe this. It's the driving theory behind the "Bright Ideas" program Studer Group urges its partner organizations to implement in order to improve

efficiency and cut costs. When you ask people to rise t
the occasion, they usually do.

So here's the bottom line: Next time you have a problem, before approaching the boss to take action to fix it, bring a possible solution (or two or three) with you. Yes, you'll need the boss's go-ahead to implement it, but if you've already got the details worked out, you'll save them a lot of work and you'll definitely speed along the process.

Imagine that you work for a Lake Mills, Wisconsin, golf club restaurant with membership options and you've noticed a problem: Because members typically purchase a monthly food and drink minimum, the last few days of every month are always jam-packed with patrons who are trying to meet the deadline. This stresses the restaurant staff and creates long waiting times and less-than-pleasant dining experiences for members.

After some careful thinking, you come up with the following solution: Rather than having everyone's billing cycle end at the end of the month, the club could stagger billing periods. Everyone whose last name begins with a letter between "A" and "D" would have a billing period that runs from the 1st of one month to the 1st of the next month. Everyone whose name falls between "F" and "H" would have a billing cycle of the 5th to the 5th. And so on and so on.

You are convinced that this idea would solve the end-of-the-month-crowd problem—so you sketch out the particulars and present it to the boss.

It's not hard to see how much more pleasant it would be for a leader to be approached with a solution like this rather than just hearing, "Everyone's showing up at the end of the month and we can't deal with it…and people are getting mad!"

Always do as much of the "heavy lifting" for the boss as you can. They will appreciate it, and the company will reap the benefits—and in the long run, so will you.

CHAPTER FIVE:

ADOPT A "NO EXCUSES" POLICY

"I attribute my success to this—I never gave or took any excuse."
—Florence Nightingale

E veryone makes mistakes. They are part of the process by which we grow as professionals and as human beings. When you think about it this way, mistakes can be a positive—assuming that you view them as learning experiences and act accordingly.

Mistakes become a problem only when we fall back on excuse making to avoid holding ourselves accountable and striving for improvement. Have you ever heard (or used) excuses like these?

"There is nothing else I could have done to help that customer. I felt bad about it but I was simply following company policy."

"Why did I miscalculate this month's billing? Well, I had too much on my plate and had to rush through the billing process…sorry."

"It's not my fault the report was turned in late. I knew the manager didn't build in enough time, but I never had a chance to tell them."

These kinds of excuses may help the employee using them rationalize why they missed a deadline or why they were rude to a customer, but they do nothing to help improve performance.

It's important to adopt what can be called a "no excuses" policy. This is a commitment you make to yourself, the boss, and your coworkers to do what you feel is in the best interests of the company and its goal of achieving excellence. It requires thinking ahead to anticipate problems and holding yourself accountable for outcomes.

Refusing to make excuses is another way of saying "I take ownership of my job and am 100 percent committed to doing my best possible work at all times." It's a mindset that fosters creative thinking and innovation. It helps you get better and better at what you do, because in the quest to avoid the need to make excuses, you naturally seek to make improvements in how you do your job. All of this, of course, can help you thrive inside the organization.

On the other hand, chronic excuse making can derail your personal progress and the progress of the organization itself. Specifically:

1. It gives you a reputation of being undependable. As a result you're less likely to be given high-priority projects, to be promoted, and to be considered for pay increases.

2. People will not want to work with you. If you work in a team project environment, coworkers will avoid having you on their team.

3. It damages future opportunities. Say you aren't fired but amicably leave your current employer. Will you really think of them as a good choice for a job reference? What if they reveal to your new potential employer your list of favorite excuses?

4. Last but not least, it harms coworkers, customers, and the entire organization. People who are always trying to excuse their own lackluster performance never try to fix the problems that are causing it...and everyone suffers.

To be clear, when you adopt a "no excuses" policy, you aren't declaring that you will never again make a mistake. Instead, you're making a pledge to think ahead and anticipate problems—and, when problems do occur, to figure out how to avoid making them again in the future.

The next time you find yourself gearing up to make an excuse to cover up a mistake, ask yourself, *Could I have foreseen this happening? If so, what could I have done differently?*

Let's say you're a customer service rep dealing with an unhappy customer. You try to appease them but it isn't working. This unwilling-to-compromise attitude gets the best of you and you let your irritation show. The customer promptly asks to speak to your manager. Could you have foreseen that outcome when you started talking with the customer? Yes—and you could have prepared for just such an event.

One option might have been to put the customer on hold. You could have given yourself a second or two to calm down and put together a list of offers you could use to improve the situation. Another option, especially if you could tell from the outset that the customer wasn't going to agree to anything you offered, would have been to ask your manager or boss to handle the call.

Or you could have armed yourself with some "key words" to access on such an occasion: "I appreciate your bringing this to my attention. What is the best approach for me to take to assure that this does not happen again?"

Of course, "experience is the best teacher" has become a cliché for a reason. We really *do* learn from experience. And that's why great employees look at their mistakes as opportunities to perfect their systems and processes. When you refuse to make excuses, you pave the way for a more effective, productive, and profitable future.

Employees who succeed (and who help their organizations succeed) do so because they are committed to giving their best each day. Adopting a "no excuses" policy will help you progress from being an undependable employee to an indispensable one.

CHAPTER SIX:

UNDERSTAND WHY CONFIDENTIALITY MATTERS

You have probably heard that transparent organizations are the best organizations. I have always found this to be true. In general, the more freely information flows from the senior executives to the mid-level managers to the staff, the better. This kind of openness builds trust, helps employees understand the *why* behind what they're being asked to do, helps them feel respected, and, in general, helps everyone do their best work.

However, it's important to remember that there will be times when your boss just can't reveal everything about other employees or the organization itself. Due to confidentiality issues, they can't legally do so.

If the boss is open and honest with you in general, please be understanding at those times when it seems they're not sharing everything they know. Don't assume they are being inauthentic or untrustworthy. *Do* assume they have a good reason for not giving you all the information at that time. Believe me, the boss wants to have your trust as much as you want to have theirs. But there will be occasions when in order to guard the trust of others, they have to protect information.

Trust the boss's judgment. When you understand the need for confidentiality, you will give your boss the benefit of the doubt when this happens, rather than assuming the worst. That will keep your relationship on solid ground.

Let's say one of your coworkers isn't performing well. They're missing deadlines, making mistakes, and becoming difficult to work with. You and others on the team probably want the boss to take action against their poor performance. It may even appear to you that the boss is being too lenient or even looking the other way.

The truth may well be that the boss is in the process of taking formal action—and is ethically obligated not to disclose that fact to the rest of the staff. That's why in certain situations when the boss says, "I'm handling it," it's best to take them at their word.

In one organization a vice president did not have the trust and respect of his employees. In fact, many of them thought he should be fired. They were frustrated and upset with the CEO for not handling the situation. But what they didn't know was that their CEO *was* handling it. He had the VP on a corrective action plan, which basically required the VP to shape up or ship out. However, because of confidentiality issues, the CEO could not share this with his employees. (Later, after the VP left, they realized he had been handling it all along.)

Build an emotional bank account. All of this illustrates why it is so essential for coworkers and leaders to build emotional bank accounts with one another. This requires doing the little things on a daily basis to create positive, productive, trust-based relationships with each other. So in order for your boss to build an emotional bank account with you, they make sure you have everything you need to do your job well and that they're available when you need to speak with them. As an employee, you build an emotional bank account by meeting deadlines, always producing your best work, showing up on time, and so forth.

When the boss is open and honest with you, they are making deposits in your emotional bank account. So on the few occasions when they have to make a "withdrawal" by keeping information confidential, there's enough trust built up that it shouldn't harm your relationship. You and others will be able to say, "There must be a good reason why we don't know or can't know." If you don't have that emotional trust built up, you're all in trouble. Relationships will stall, and people will assume the worst.

Years ago, I found out an employee had done some things that were inappropriate, and we were going to have to let him go. As we were working out his departure, he asked for a severance package and we said, "No." We felt that doing so would have gone against our values. The employee then said that if we didn't give him a severance package he would go out into the community, where he was well-known, and tell people his side of the story.

Now, there was no way we could have told our side of the story because we were bound by confidentiality issues. The good news is that we had built up trust in the community so when this former employee tried to turn people against us, his story did not get any traction, and he actually hurt his own reputation and eventually left the community altogether.

That's the power of an emotional bank account. We couldn't explain ourselves fully to our employees or the community, but because we had a reputation for always providing information whenever we could, people did not turn against us.

Understand the boss's obligations. Now, let's talk about the other side of the confidentiality coin. Sometimes when you ask the boss for confidentiality they won't be able to provide it. For example, when I was president of an organization I did lunches with the employees, and often someone would eventually say, "What is said here stays here."

Of course I wanted them to trust me, and these meetings were actually vital in building that trust. But I knew certain things might be said that, as president, I wouldn't be able to keep confidential. I began starting each meeting by saying, "I cannot guarantee you total confidentiality. I will do everything I can to keep what is discussed here confidential, but if I hear something that I need to take action on—be it a legal issue, an ethical issue, or a values-based issue—please understand I have a responsibility to do so."

Very rarely did anything come up that fit that description, but I couldn't promise confidentiality knowing that I may have to break it if something did come up.

Here's the bottom line: It's important to be understanding of the responsibilities the boss has and how those responsibilities might affect their relationship with you and others. Discuss with them the confidentiality guidelines they must follow so that you know what can and can't be kept confidential. And in those rare situations in which your boss can't keep something you've told them confidential—because it might put you, your employees, or the organization in danger—trust them to handle the situation appropriately.

Also make sure you understand what their and your responsibilities are regarding customer confidentiality. Some information must be kept confidential in order to preserve those relationships—for instance, anything regarding customer pricing, intellectual capital, product use, and so forth. Your boss can provide guidance in this area.

Protect the boss's trust. Finally, if your boss does happen to share a piece of information with you, take it as a big compliment and guard it with your life. Revealing it to anyone, even your best friend at work who swears never to tell, can shatter many years' worth of trust.

It's important to protect the trust you have with your leaders. Mutual trust is the basis of great relationships in the workplace. Once broken, it can't be fully repaired.

CHAPTER SEVEN:

KNOW THE
BOSS'S *WHAT*

D o you want to make your workdays smoother, easier, and more productive? Most of us do. And there's a secret to achieving this goal that does not require a huge change in behavior. Learn what really matters to your boss—what their *what* is, in other words—and really laser-focus on meeting their needs in this area. It will make their job better, and that, in turn, will make *yours* better.

The best way to explain the *what* principle is this: Everyone has one or two defining actions or attributes that outweigh all others in their mind. That includes you. Maybe your *what* happens to be punctuality. You just can't stand it when people aren't on time or when deadlines get missed. It ruins your whole day and keeps you from doing your best work.

Well, the boss has a *what* as well. Maybe theirs is that people proactively tell them when something goes wrong, rather than leaving them to hear about it later. Or maybe it's positivity—hearing employees griping, complaining, and expecting the worst pushes the boss's buttons like nothing else.

When you know the boss's *what* and pay attention to it, you're able to create a productive relationship with them. When you understand what makes the boss tick—and what makes them crazy—you can work with them smoothly and efficiently. They'll be happier with your work and quite frankly they'll like you more.

The best news is that it doesn't require a huge shift in your behavior—it's probably a matter of making a few tweaks in what you're already doing.

Of course, you won't be able to make the boss happy 100 percent of the time. It's not humanly possible. But when you know what matters most to them, you *will* be able to consistently meet and surpass their expectations—and this can have a dramatic positive effect on your own work life.

By the way, this is not meant to be a self-serving exercise. Yes, it will benefit you in many ways. But it will also benefit the boss, your coworkers, and the entire organization.

Here are a few things to consider when striving to meet the boss's *whats*:

Pay attention. Who in your organization seems to have the smoothest, most productive working relationships with the boss? What are these people doing that seems to strike a chord with them? When has the boss been most pleased with your performance—and what led to this approval? On the other hand, what sorts of actions or behaviors seem to irritate them? Be mindful of these patterns and their implications. It's amazing what you can learn when you simply pay attention.

You don't have to guess. Just ask. If you've been avoiding asking the boss about their *what* because you're afraid they'll think you have no idea what you're doing, put your mind at ease. They will almost certainly appreciate any effort you put into making their job easier and your department as a whole run more smoothly. Simply ask, "What is the one area that you would most like me to place an extra focus on?" Then, take the answer to heart. By asking, you take the guesswork out of your job and ensure that you are attacking those tasks that matter most to the boss—and in the manner they find most helpful.

Keep in mind that there are also secondary *whats*—and these can change. Your boss's primary *whats* are more permanent—they're associated with their character, work style, and personal preferences. But they have secondary *whats* too, and these change depending on what's going on in your organization's external environment and what kind of pressure the boss is under. Recognize what is going on in today's external environment. Understand that things are constantly changing and learn how those changes will affect the boss and the organization as a whole.

For example, sometimes their secondary *what* might be doing everything you can to reduce expenses. Other times it might be following an initiative put in place to improve customer satisfaction. The bottom line is that you'll want to follow up frequently with your boss to find out their *what* of the month or year.

Ask the boss how you can help them deliver on *their* boss's *whats*. It's very likely that your boss has their own set of higher-ups to answer to, and those higher-ups have *whats* of their own. Ask how you can help them deliver on those tasks and initiatives that are important to their boss. This will provide you with yet another opportunity to form a great working relationship with them and to put in great work that earns their respect.

One way to do this might be to make suggestions as to what tasks you can take off the boss's plate. For example, offer to handle finding an employee to cover the shift of someone who has called in sick. Or tell them you'll be happy to start ordering supplies so they no longer have to. When you make suggestions, the boss can give you quick approval, and then get back to work delivering on their boss's *whats*.

Spread the word. More likely than not, delivering on the boss's *what* is going to take more than one person. That's why it is so important that you get others on board. Inform them about your boss's *what* and work with them to find ways to meet it. Also, warn them if they're about to violate a *what*—you'll be doing them a valuable service.

It's the pursuit of the *whats*—for both bosses and employees—that moves organizations from good to great. When you know each other's *whats*, you can better meet one another's needs. And when that starts happening, everything gets better and better.

Get the *Whats* in Writing

You might suggest to the boss that they write down what matters most to them. I do this for employees at Studer Group. I find that they appreciate knowing exactly what I expect from them and how I prefer them to work. Here is a document that I distribute to all employees:

How to work with Quint:

1. **Show me materials very early in the process.** Fancy is not good. Material does not need to be in covers, slick, illustrated with graphs, etc. I like to see things early so we can discuss if you are on the right track. This works like a GPS. If looked at early, the driver can stay on the right road. If we wait too long to check the GPS, the driver and passengers can be lost, and it can take extra time and money to get back on track.

2. **Be specific.** Don't generalize by saying things such as "The coaches are saying..." Do not generalize. We teach other leaders not to accept it and I won't. It's better to coach

people on specific problems *as they occur* than to wait three months and say, "You never do such and such…" When we're specific and when we act in the moment, we have a much better chance of fixing the problem.

3. **Act like an owner.** Spend money like it is yours.

4. **Bring a solution.** Pointing out a problem is better than not pointing out a problem. Don't wait to be led. For example, a coach recently showed me a much-improved system for orienting new staff. I loved it. She was not asked to do this; she just was thinking about how introducing new team members to SG policies, materials, tools, and processes could be done better. She wrote her ideas on a piece of paper and said, "What do you think?" This to me is excellent leadership.

5. **Write me if you have a question.** One day I received two e-mails that were about what to do if an organization is not showing gains in patient satisfaction. This allowed me to write my thoughts to many in a tip fashion. So by sharing my written response, each coach can help many. (Just please follow up

with a phone call if you don't hear back from me within 24 hours.)

6. **If I ask for comments, questions, and/ or concerns, while you don't need to respond every time, do respond when you can.** This helps me know if the message was received and if the receivers understand or want to share their own viewpoints. For example, on an expense note, four people wrote me with ideas they feel would work or with concerns on what may come. These were helpful. Sadly, many of you have never responded. I notice.

7. **Tell me some positives about SG and most importantly our people.** Trust me: I usually hear what is wrong, who spent too much, who did not complete an assignment, etc. I need the 3-to-1 "positive-to-negative" ratio just like everyone else. Plus, I pass the positives on to others.

8. **Say it early.** Make your main point, suggestions, or return on investment statement in the first sentence on notes to me.

9. **Don't wait.** If you are going to not make a deadline or miss a target, or if you have an

issue, tell me. It is better for me to be told by you than to realize it later. For example, if a 90-day plan is due and you have not turned it in, you know it. If I have to ask, then I am thinking, *What else have they not done and not said anything about?* It creates anxiety. Talk to anyone who has worked with me a long time and you will find that saying something is much better than waiting to see what happens. If the results are not there, say something. Maybe we can help.

10. **Think and communicate horizontally.** This is a difficult one. By this I mean if you are doing something that is working, ask yourself, *How can I show this to others at SG who may find it helpful?* This is called teamwork. Also, you may find you have a tool, technique, or system that will help others.

11. **Control your own destiny.** If you feel we are not talking enough, call me. Ask questions. When it's convenient and cost effective, shadow me.

12. **Come to me directly.** At times I find people will tell someone I talk to often something in hopes that the other person will tell me. It's best to carry our own messages.

13. Keep me in the loop on material and work. Not that I am checking, but I can sometimes use what you're doing in talks or in helping others or in pointing out what you can send to others to help them achieve success.

Chapter Eight:

Don't Feel Qualified? Ask for Training

T raining counts. Most leaders realize that it's just smart business to make sure people at all levels have the skills they need to do their jobs effectively. Unfortunately, when money gets tight and costs are being cut, skill development is often one of the first things to go. And the irony is that when times are tough and fewer employees are asked to do more with fewer resources, training is more important than ever.

I've worked inside organizations where people are promoted to the next level of leadership with no training. (I've seen this in healthcare quite a bit, but it happens in all industries.) And it's just a fact of life that when people aren't trained for the job they're moving into, they're going to struggle.

In a perfect world, effective training programs would be hardwired into all organizations. It's the only way to make sure employees, from top to bottom, can meet organizational goals while improving their own "personal best." But sometimes training isn't automatically offered—and that's when it's up to employees to step up and seek it out on their own.

I find that the best employees do this, anyway. Their sense of ownership tells them that they, not the organization, are ultimately responsible for their own development.

Asking for training makes you more likely to get it. You might find that it's not a money issue at all—maybe the boss truly doesn't realize you need it. If you can make them understand that training will enable you to get things done more quickly and efficiently, chances are they'll help you get the skills you need. And obviously, having the right skill set benefits the company—and you—in numerous ways.

Here's the point: When you see that you need training to do your job better—or decide you want it in order to advance to the next level—don't wait for the boss to ask. Get proactive about getting some. Here are a few suggestions:

Come right out and ask for it. Don't be afraid. The boss will view you as a solid performer and will appreciate that you are actively seeking ways to improve your performance and the organization. To start the dialogue, ask if the two of you can take some time to review your goals and priorities. During this conversation make the boss aware that you are ready to take on new responsibilities and ask how you can receive the training and coaching necessary in order to do them well. (You might also bring this up during your performance eval.)

Of course, it's important to be aware that the boss might say no. If this happens, you may feel rejected. Try not to take it personally. There could be any number of valid reasons for the no. Perhaps the boss feels you're too valuable in your current role, or there's no budget for training, or from their perspective you simply aren't ready. What you *can* do is state that you'd like them to revisit your request later. Most good bosses want their employees to be happy and will do everything possible to accommodate your wish—even if it doesn't happen on your timetable.

Remember, it's never too late for proper training. As I mentioned earlier, many people are thrust into leadership positions with virtually no training at all. In healthcare they start out with a precursor for a job title—"Interim." It's a common situation: A leader quits and the organization needs to move quickly to fill the position. So they appoint someone as the "interim" leader. Over time that person becomes the permanent leader, only they've never received the training needed to do the job as effectively as possible.

If you find yourself in this situation, know that you don't have to simply go along with the status quo because you have held a position for six months or more. The boss might think everything is fine—after all, nothing's gone wrong so far—but if you're drowning in the new responsibilities, it is okay to speak up.

Whether you've come from a non-leadership position into a leadership position or whether you've simply taken on new responsibilities, it's never too late to receive training that will help you do your job more efficiently and effectively. Ask the boss for help. Seek out the training you need.

Take full advantage of the training that you do get. Understand that the point isn't to get trained— it's the outcomes that result from the training. It doesn't matter if you enjoyed a training session if 90 days later you are still getting the same results. Be sure to focus on specific outcomes. Measure your results. If you aren't satisfied, revisit what you were taught in the training sessions and reassess how you are implementing those lessons. After training, send your supervisor a note on your learnings.

Find a mentor. If formal leadership training isn't available at your company, perhaps you could seek out a mentor. Seek out professional development opportunities, often asking for mentorship or additional training to advance your career. Identify a possible mentor for yourself and your own professional growth and development as an employee or leader. This might be someone in the organization in the same role as you, but it could also be a person in a position you aspire to. (Maybe it could even be the boss…you'll never know if you don't ask.)

Realize that training doesn't have to be expensive. Sure, these days you can spend a lot of money on quality training. There are multi-day seminars and conferences that can set you back thousands of dollars, and there are off-site training programs that require a week of your time and a hefty sum of money. But learning valuable skills doesn't have to cost a small fortune.

Quality training also comes in many other, less expensive forms. There are inexpensive or free webinars and podcasts and many great books and articles on pretty much every topic you could need.

Maintain a balance. Sometimes people get so wrapped up in their new training that they get distracted from their day-to-day responsibilities. Just remember, you won't be helping the boss or anyone else by pursuing more training if others have to pick up your slack. Carefully plan your training time. Read a training book during your lunch break, listen to a podcast on your way to work, or attend a night (or off-shift) class. Once you are confident with what you've learned, you can begin implementing it.

When you do get training, share it with coworkers. Some organizations make it a requirement that when people do get training they find two or three points to formally share with coworkers. This is a great idea as it allows many people to benefit from one person's training—especially important in a challenging economy. If this isn't mandatory at your company, offer to do it anyway. The boss will appreciate your initiative.

Great employees are proactive about training. They seek it out, advocate for it, or find ways to receive it on their own. The right training helps them do their jobs better, shows that they are striving to constantly improve, and proves they are high performers who can handle whatever is thrown at them.

It's that kind of initiative and drive that make you a valuable asset to an organization—and in turn, make that organization work best for you.

CHAPTER NINE:

MEET DEADLINES. IF YOU SEE YOU WON'T, SAY SO EARLY

I t is easy to think of deadlines as a "necessary evil" because of the stress associated with them. But really, they don't have to be. Deadlines are what make business happen. They are the life's blood of an organization. Missing them can bottleneck an entire project.

Not only do they keep things running smoothly and ensure that key tasks are completed, well-spaced deadlines motivate people and sharpen their thinking.

When deadlines are met, not only are we doing our part to keep the organization healthy (and customers happy!), it makes life easier for leaders and others who count on us. It's just good for our brand.

And yet, we all fall short of this goal at times. Despite our best efforts, interruptions, fires that must be put out, and unexpected tasks that take precedence mean that sometimes deadlines are missed. It happens.

So how best to handle it when you know you're going to miss one? To me, the answer boils down to two simple rules:

1. Let the boss know as soon as possible that the deadline will be missed.

2. Learn from the experience—put systems in place to make it less likely to happen again.

Let's talk about Rule 1 first. Tell the boss as early in the process as you can. They may be able to provide solutions to help you get back on track. At the very least you'll provide them with the opportunity to inform customers or higher-ups that the project will require a little extra time so that they can adjust accordingly.

I find that many people dread giving their boss the bad news. Consequently, they wait so long to tell them that by the time they do they've missed the window of opportunity in which they could have called in more support or helped meet the deadline in some other way.

A good boss isn't going to be angry with you for missing a deadline—especially when you've really worked hard to meet it. In fact, they will appreciate your keeping the lines of communication open. And nine times out of ten they'd rather you be realistic about it than try to rush it in under the wire and do poor quality work.

Now for Rule 2: Actively look for ways to avoid missing more deadlines in the future. Here are a few suggestions:

Be realistic about how long a task will take. (And tell the boss!) Let's say you are tasked with compiling a report. What you can do is look back and determine how long similar tasks took in the past. This will help you realize "Okay, I need to carve out two and a half full days to do this work." Then, you'll need to figure out where those two and a half days are going to come from, taking into account all the other projects on your plate, any upcoming time off like holidays, doctor appointments, and so forth. This will allow you to come up with a realistic deadline.

Next, share all this information with the boss. They may have no idea how long what they're asking you to do actually takes. (Why would they, especially if they've never done it themselves?) And always remember: The time to negotiate a deadline is when it is given, *not* when it is due. If the task will be hard to complete, you may need to ask for more time upfront or suggest other items that may be taken off your plate to allow you to focus on this new one.

Break the project into sections with deadlines. Force yourself to commit to them. Think of it as setting mini-goals with the project's completion being your ultimate goal. Create reminders for yourself around the deadlines. (You can write them in your planner, or if you're a high-tech type, make use of a computer reminder program.)

It's best not to spend too long agonizing over the first chapter. You might give yourself, say, a week to bring it to completion. There is something about finishing up that first chunk of work that gives you a psychological push and makes it much easier to work on the rest of the book.

Don't worry about getting every chapter perfect. The important thing is to stick to your timeline. Most likely the chapters will be at 80 percent on the first go around, and on the final read-through you can move them to 100 percent. (I'm a big believer in "progress over perfection"!)

Get organized. Before you jump into any project, take some time to get organized. Clean up your work area. Get rid of any excess stuff that may have stuck around after your last project. Then make sure you have everything you need to complete this one. If you are going to need a team of people to help you complete the project, get the team together at this point. Go through each step of the project and figure out who should do what.

Make a list and check it twice. Checklists and to-do lists can be invaluable when you are working under a deadline. If you're juggling multiple projects, they're absolutely necessary. A checklist will ensure you've consulted everyone needed for a certain step in your project and that you and your team have everything necessary to complete the day's work. A to-do list helps you keep up with all the little things that must be accomplished in order for you to meet your deadline—and helps you keep track of all the tasks that you still must complete that *aren't* connected to your deadlined project.

Anticipate problems. You can do your best to avoid problems and hang-ups, but it is unlikely that you will be able to dodge them all. Anything could go wrong.

A key player might be out sick on a day when a big deliverable is due. The boss might unexpectedly push up the deadline. Your computer might crash. Anticipating problems allows you to at least consider what your contingency plan might be if something goes wrong. That way, you'll be able to find a solution and get back on track much faster.

Prioritize. When putting together your day's to-do list, organize tasks by level of importance. Put the most important tasks at the top of your list and try to knock those out first. If you ever find that you aren't sure what is a more important part of a project, ask the boss. They expect to provide guidance when you need it and may have the perspective you need in order to make the right prioritization decisions.

Regularly touch base with the boss. Keeping them up to date on where you are in the process will enable them to help you prioritize other tasks. Sometimes what you think is a hard deadline may really be a "soft" deadline. By checking in with the boss regularly you give them the opportunity to redirect you if you're spending too much time on one project and neglecting others (which might be more important).

Enlist help whenever possible. You don't have to go every project alone. The best way to meet a deadline is often to get a team of people together to help. (Get the boss's permission first, of course!) When it makes sense to do so, delegate tasks to others. Let them know the project's deadline and ask them to prioritize accordingly. Enlisting a few helping hands will help keep you on track and will very likely make the project a more rewarding task.

Meeting deadlines shows that you are truly committed to your job rather than just going through the motions. It reflects the kind of mindset that makes you a valuable employee, a good coworker, and part of an organization that customers can trust and count on.

CHAPTER TEN:

IF YOU HAVE A BEST PRACTICE OR BETTER WAY, SHARE IT

I'm sure you've heard the saying that imitation is the sincerest form of flattery. And according to the *Harvard Business Review*, it is also good for business. Oded Shenkar's *Defend Your Research* feature titled "Imitation Is More Valuable Than Innovation" made the case that finding really good ideas developed by others and copying them is a major source of progress for organizations.

Shenkar's article reveals that 97.8 percent of the value of innovations goes to imitators! In fact, some of the world's most successful businesses are actually "copycats." For example, McDonald's imitated a system developed by White Castle. And Visa, MasterCard, and American Express all followed in the footsteps of Diner's Club.

We at Studer Group certainly believe in the importance of imitation. In fact, harvesting and moving best practices is a form of "imitation" we've advocated for years. Harvesting best practices means taking what people are doing right—people in other organizations, yes, but also people in other areas of our *own* organizations—and expanding it.

Why are best practices so valuable? The simple answer is that they keep us from having to reinvent the wheel. Implementing techniques and processes that have already been proven to work decreases the amount of time we have to spend figuring out and solving problems. It's so much more effective than trying to start from scratch—and it builds goodwill and a stronger company.

My own work with companies across the country has shown me that applying best practices makes organizations far more effective and efficient. It also saves a lot of money and generates tremendous revenue. That's why we teach leaders to keep a sharp eye out for colleagues or employees who might be doing an exceptional job at, say, closing sales or motivating people or smoothing the ruffled feathers of upset customers.

That said, if you've figured out a way to do your job better, faster, or more effectively than others in your company, don't wait for the boss to ask about your secret—take the initiative and tell them. Not only will you help your organization get better, you'll improve your personal brand and show that you're a fully engaged employee.

I find that no one is better at solving problems than the people who deal with those problems every day. Necessity usually drives innovation. That's why it's not surprising that organizations are filled with people who've figured out "a better way."

Unfortunately I also find that few employees share their best practices. Some don't realize that their coworkers have the same problems as them. Others are too modest and don't want to seem like they are showing off or trying to be the boss's favorite. And there are even a few who don't want to lose the competitive edge that they feel their best practices give them over coworkers.

I urge you to overcome any resistance you may feel and share your best practices with the boss. But don't stop there—also offer your thoughts on how to transfer what you do best to others in the organization. Here's how:

Figure out what you do best. Can others benefit from your best practice? Maybe you have a client follow-up method that always yields results or maybe you've developed a personal filing system that keeps you organized and helps you work more efficiently. Don't assume the boss already knows about it— they probably don't. Whatever your best practices are, think about how coworkers and the company as a whole would benefit if they were used throughout the organization.

Don't be overly modest. Remember, you're helping the company, not bragging! This helps you and others have more job security. Don't minimize what you do by saying, "Oh, it's no big deal." The reality is your best practices can have a huge positive impact on your organization, and that's something to be proud of, not to avoid.

Share all the details with the boss. Get your best practice down on paper. Detail how it works for you and how it improves the way you work. Don't forget to mention how it will help the company. Will it lower expenses? Provide better customer service? Boost productivity? Create happier employees? Communicate the *why* clearly and often. This will help the boss when they explain your best practice to others in the organization.

Offer to help train others. Best practices rarely translate seamlessly from one person to another or one department to another. They simply aren't always a perfect fit. Always feel free to make suggestions on how to move your best practice to other employees or departments. And let the boss know that you are willing to help others transition into using your best practice by being an integral part of the training process.

Keep searching. Never stop looking for the next great way to do something. Don't limit yourself to only telling the boss about your best practices. If you read an article about a best practice at another company that you think your organization would benefit from, show the article to the boss. Or if a friend tells you about one of their best practices, share it. Keeping your eyes and ears open for best practices is a great way to show the boss that you think of yourself as an "owner" at your organization.

Organizations that harvest and move best practices *consistently* get great outcomes. Moving best practices yields better outcomes—and creates a better place for you, coworkers, and leaders to work and provides a better service to your customers.

Make it your mission to do whatever you can to create an organization that consistently performs at the highest possible level. Never stop looking for best practic es to harvest and implement—they're your key to success in a rapidly changing world.

Chapter Eleven:

If You're Wondering about the *Why*, Ask

A t every organization, decisions are made every day. They may center on how to improve customer service...or how to manage employees in an expanding workforce...or how to keep morale high with a staff reduction...or how to out-innovate the competition in a tough economy. All of these decisions have major implications—and most of them will, at some point or other, trickle down to employees like you.

Some of these decisions likely make perfect sense to you and your coworkers. For example, it's easy to see why your organization might want to implement the use of a project management system or overhaul the shipping and receiving processes to make sure customer orders are sent out more quickly.

Other times, though, it may not be so clear why the organization is doing what it's doing. When that's the case people may jump to the wrong conclusion—often assuming the "worst case scenario"—and send rumors ying around. Complaining and finger pointing may flourish. As negativity becomes the norm, morale may take a nosedive.

Or, because they misinterpret what's driving a particular change, people may take it upon themselves to start doing things a "better way." They think they're helping, but instead they're unknowingly hurting the cause.

All this damage can be averted by making sure you and others understand the *why*. Yes, it would be best if the boss told you upfront, but if they don't, it's up to you to ask.

Yes, you may feel slightly uncomfortable asking *why* to a non-communicative leader. I urge you to do it anyway. You'll probably find that the boss actually appreciates that you're being the "squeaky wheel" (in a very positive way).

Making a point to find out the *why* and share it with others keeps organizations running smoothly. It soothes anxiety and keeps the workplace positive. It helps eliminate we/theyism and unifies the company. That's because when employees understand the *why*, rumors that cast higher-ups in a less-than-flattering light are less likely to pop up. Others may come to see their work environment with a fresh eye…and they may find this new perspective inspiring.

Knowing the *why* also keeps you (and your coworkers) connected to the purpose of your work (e.g., serving customer needs). It's when you feel this connection that you are motivated to do what needs to be done to serve customers, fellow team members, and the entire orga-zation.

Let's say you've just found out that your department is to start providing weekly customer satisfaction reports. If you react by commenting that the higher-ups must think your department isn't performing well and someone must be getting the ax, you'll harm morale and end up hurting your own credibility and trustworthiness. But if you go to your manager and ask *why*, the story may turn out quite differently.

For example, you might find out the higher-ups have received great feedback from customers about your de-partment and they implemented the reporting system to figure out a way to spread your department's best practic-es throughout the organization. So yes, your department was being singled out...but for good reasons, not bad.

So how do you go about finding out the *why?* A few points to consider:

Evaluate values. Before you assume the worst about the possible *why* behind a decision, consider the values that may have influenced it. You may already know that customers like when your company proactively provides feedback and product updates. Therefore, you can prob-ably safely assume the change you're being asked to make will accomplish these goals even more effectively. Once you discover that's true, your values won't allow you *not* to make the change.

Ask the boss to be specific. Part of the boss's job is to help you and your coworkers connect to the *why*. When you feel more explanation is needed to really drive point home, ask for specifics. For example, suppose you are being asked to supply customer surveys to your clients, which ask specific questions about their location, demographics, etc. Your boss delivers this request, and says, "It will really be a big help."

While you don't doubt that it will be, maybe you feel that knowing more about the *why* will help you do a better job. Ask the boss to be a little more specific. You'll probably hear that the company wants to expand in locations and industries where it already has other customers. Knowing this information will not only help you and others in the company do your jobs better, it will also help you take pride in what you do.

Help them make it a priority to share the *why*. Getting in touch with the *why* behind what you do can be a powerful experience. Studer Group recently surveyed one of our clients' employees, asking when their supervisors last shared a note, a story, or an example of how an individual, a department, or the organization made a positive impact on its customers. Only 1 percent of the employees said they had heard a story of this nature in the last 90 days. When is the last time you heard such a story?

Sometimes it is easy for employees and leaders alike to get so caught up in running an organization that they neglect to stop and think about why what they are doing is important. Remind your boss often that you and your coworkers want and need to hear about the *why* and that it helps keep everyone aligned in a common sense of purpose. You might even suggest a few ways they can keep the *why* in front of everyone in the organization via newsletters, employee forums, and so forth.

Chances are, the boss wants people to be informed about everything going on in your department and any other decisions affecting you. If they don't explicitly explain the *why* behind a decision, it's likely because a) they're too busy, b) they assume you already know, or c) both of the above. If you can help the boss communicate the *why* to others, they will most likely be grateful.

Finally, don't feed the rumor mill. (In fact, shut it down when you can.) When you do hear rumors about what's going on with the company, dispel them if at all possible. If you understand the *why* behind a certain initiative, but coworkers aren't seeing it, explain it to them. And if you think they aren't heeding your input, then it's time to bring in the boss. Explain to them that certain rumors have popped up that could lead to bigger problems. When the boss knows this, they should quickly take action in explaining the *why* to provide perspective and dispel snowballing rumors.

Taking the initiative to find out what you need to know—and sharing that knowledge with others—will go a long way toward creating a positive, productive, passion-driven workplace. You'll not only bring peace of mind to yourself and others who were curious about a given decision, you'll show the boss that you're a fully engaged employee. They'll see that you really care about what you're doing…and why.

CHAPTER TWELVE:

BE A GOOD COMMUNICATOR

H*ow well do you communicate with the boss?*
It's an important question. How you communicate is the lens through which the boss views you and your contributions. Their perception of you *is* their reality. It's possible that you're routinely working at exceeding customers' and coworkers' expectations—but unless you're communicating properly with the boss, they may not realize what a great job you're doing.

Many people assume that it's the boss's responsibility to drive communication. *If the boss has a question for me, they'll ask,* they reason. *I'm too busy doing my job to worry about constantly checking in with them.* But I find the best and most successful employees take the opposite approach: They make it a priority to stay in contact with the boss.

In reality, the boss may be too busy and pulled in too many different directions to keep up with exactly what you are doing at any given time. That's why it's best to sume that they don't know—and to assume the "communication" ball is always in your court.

Being a good communicator means making sure the boss knows what's going on in your corner of the world. Receiving regular feedback from you on projects you're working on will help the boss determine how to move forward with clients and customers. And hearing from you on other workplace issues will help them understand how to better meet your needs and those of others inside the organization.

Communicating proactively with the boss will make you more effective at your job. It will help ensure that you're putting your energy toward the right projects. Remember, priorities can change—and by regularly "checking in" you can make sure that what the boss said mattered last week *still* matters this week!

Also, of course, staying in front of the boss ensures that they know what you've accomplished. This will serve you well when it's time for your performance eval!

Read on for some advice on how you can be a great communicator:

Don't under-communicate. This is a common mistake made by people who don't want to overwhelm, interrupt, or "bother" the boss with too much information. It may also be a practice of introverts or shy individuals who feel uncomfortable being "in the spotlight" with the boss. Try not to make the "under-communicating" mistake. While you don't have to tell the boss every single detail about your progress on a certain project or your sales call with a new client, it is important to keep them "in the loop."

It's probably a good idea to send the boss e-mail updates, whether they ask for them or not. Look for opportunities to drop in for a face-to-face conversation (if you work in the same location) or at least to pick up the phone and call. And update the boss at all key stages of important projects.

Not sure if you're striking the right balance between over-communicating and under-communicating? Just ask. Specifically, ask the boss a) how often they'd like to hear from you, and b) what level of detail they'd like. Then, work hard to honor their requests.

Respond to the boss in a timely manner. When the boss calls or sends an e-mail, get back quickly—the same day, if possible, or at least within 24 hours. If they're calling with a question, you don't have to have the answer the minute you call back. And if the boss is e-mailing you about a project, chances are they're not expecting you to send it to them that second. They just want to know you got the message and are working on it—that assurance will relieve anxiety and let them know you're attuned to their priorities.

When you ask the boss for something, get a "response timeline" from them as well. This is a reasonable request and most leaders are happy to provide an answer. Knowing when the boss is likely to get back to you with the information you need helps you plan and prioritize, yes…but it also helps them.

Know when to e-mail and when to call. There's a time and place for both, of course, but many people today have taken to sending e-mails almost all the time. Sometimes they do it to avoid conversations that might put them on the spot. Other times, it just seems easier—and faster—to e-mail than to get into a long conversation. But e-mail can't do everything: Sometimes there's no substitute for the "give and take" of a phone call.

Let's say a complicated project has been stalled due to a misunderstanding between you and a client. You need to let the boss know in order to keep them in the loop, but you also want advice on how best to handle the situation. The details of what happened may be too complicated to communicate via the back and forth of e-mail, but a relatively brief phone conversation could clear everything right up.

A good rule of thumb is this: When in doubt, pick up the phone. The boss will appreciate your commitment to clearly communicating issues even when they might put you in the line of fire. Keep in mind, too, that clear communication in these situations will give the boss confidence that you use quality communication skills with your clients and coworkers.

Observe basic e-mail etiquette. Many people, whether they lead others or not, are unaware of the basic "rules" of courteous e-mailing. You might consider reading up on this subject. In a global workplace, more and more people communicate with the boss almost only by e-mail. That means the e-mails you compose *are* you in the boss's mind. A few pointers:

- Be brief and succinct. Write in short sentences. one wants to read long, rambling blocks of text (a. certainly not busy leaders).

- When replying to an e-mail, answer all questions. If you don't, you'll force the boss to have to send another e-mail. In fact, get in the habit of anticipating questions they may ask and answer them ahead of time.

- Don't write in all caps. Not only is it hard to read, it looks like you're shouting.

- Everything is not high priority. If you overuse this feature, you'll be like the little boy who cried wolf too many times.

- Before you send it, read it again. And again. Once you hit "send" it's too late to take it back.

Know who to CC (and who not to CC). We've all been CCed on an e-mail or two before and wondered, *Why do I need to know about this?* Sometimes CCing others on e-mails can be an easy and quick way to keep everyone, including the boss, in the loop. The trouble is it's so easy that sometimes we overdo it. Before CCing anyone, always ask yourself, *Does this person really need this information?* And then ask yourself, *Would it be better to deliver this information over the phone?*

Generally, CCing others is effective when you have to send one message to several people. It's also a good way to keep the boss informed about where you are on important projects or to show that you did indeed take care of something you said you'd handle. Just make sure the message is something the boss will want to know about that you aren't clogging up their or anyone else's mailbox. (Again, asking the boss about their communication preferences in general will allow you to make a pretty safe guess.)

Always give the boss the unvarnished truth. Know that the boss doesn't expect or want you to candy coat the information you give them or put a (false) positive "spin" on any data you're sharing. Sometimes what you have to say might not be music to the boss's ears—for example, if an expensive piece of equipment has broken down and needs replacement or if there's been a mistake with a big customer order—but respect that they can handle the hard truth.

Be open and honest when you communicate with the boss. Get straight to the point and you'll both be able to start reaching a positive solution much more quickly.

Speak up when everyone else is clamming up. In many workplaces people avoid telling the boss what they know in their heart of hearts they need to hear. Oh, they may not lie, but they also might not volunteer critical information.

In general, if rumors or gossip are going around that you think the boss may want to address, tell them about it. If they ask for direct and honest feedback—even if it has to do with their performance or other sensitive matters—give it. Don't withhold information simply because you are afraid of rocking the boat or because you don't want to draw any attention to yourself. Sometimes, and especially in professional situations, being a great communicator means being the one guy (or gal) who's willing to speak up.

When you need to have an important conversation with the boss, prepare ahead of time. Think through what you want to say and make sure it all makes sense. Anticipate what the boss might say so you can be prepared to address their concerns. It's often a good idea to jot down some talking points to refer to so you won't "blank" at a critical moment or forget something important. Preparation is helpful for everyone, but it's especially helpful for introverts who really need to think through issues before they can talk about them.

Know what your body language is saying. You can be *saying* all the right words, but your body language might not always back them up. For example, have you ever missed out on being chosen as point person for an important project and wondered why? It could be that while you thought you were successfully expressing your abilities to the boss or a client, your body language— crossed arms, hunched shoulders, lack of eye contact— were betraying a lack of confidence to the decision makers.

Body language is essential in the workplace because it plays a huge role in how others perceive you. It determines whether they think you come from a position of power, whether they think they can trust you, and whether they respect you. Use the wrong body language and you can create subtle anxiety or distrust in others. Use the right body language and it might help you get that promotion, close the deal, or strengthen a relationship.

Start paying closer attention to what you're doing with your body during conversations with the boss and others at work. Don't cross your arms or fidget as these movements can make you look less confident or even uninterested. Instead, focus on standing (or sitting) up straight, making eye contact, and using appropriate hand gestures to emphasize important points. When you become fluent in great body language, you'll be able to strengthen your connections with others, which will certainly give you a boost in the workplace.

Be informed. Part of being a great communicator is knowing what *not* to say. Know what's going on so that you don't ask unnecessary questions or give the boss outdated information. Read the company's newsletters, communication boards, and so forth and stay up to date on what is going on in your industry. Pay attention at staff meetings and ask for clarification anytime you need it. By staying in tune with everything going on in your department, organization, and industry, you'll have a better understanding of what does and doesn't need to be communicated.

In large part, being a great communicator is powerful precisely because it's such a rare quality. Make it your mission to communicate well at work, *especially* with the boss. When you are able to master this skill you'll build a stronger, more productive relationship with them—and that will make your work life easier, more productive, and far more rewarding.

Section Two:

Working Best with Your Coworkers

CHAPTER THIRTEEN:

STAMP OUT WE/THEYISM

*I*t's *not us! It's them!* This complaint can be heard in organizations of all shapes and sizes. In fact, it might be the unofficial motto of organizations that have been infected with we/theyism.

What is we/theyism? Basically, it's making oneself look better at the expense of others. And unfortunately, it can seriously harm organizations from top to bottom: dividing employees and leaders...creating animosity between departments...causing a complete breakdown in teamwork and mutual respect.

We/theyism seems to be the "default setting" for many workforces. We do it because we've never been taught *not* to do it. The great news is it can be overcome—and when it is, the results can be dramatic.

People will perform better and actually enjoy working together. People will take ownership of problems and opportunities, which keeps the organization constantly moving forward. The result is a more positive company culture that allows people at every level to thrive, and that makes for happier, better-served customers.

We/theyism can happen at every level. It's often a method leaders don't even realize they are doing. For example, if an employee comes to a manager upset because they did not get a raise that reflected all the hard work they had put in that year, the manager might say, "I can certainly understand how you feel. If it were up to me, it wouldn't have been like that. But you know pay raises are really out of my hands. That's something that Human Resources dictates." Many times this way of communicating has been in an organization for decades.

It's true that this conversation may have made the employee like the manager more, but at what cost? Now the employee feels adversarial toward another department or leader! It would have been better to say something like "We work very hard to have a fair compensation system. Let me review how it works. This may not change your mind; however, I feel the system is a fair one."

It's important to note that we/theyism is not just an issue that leaders have to deal with; it's a phenomenon that affects *everyone* at an organization. We've all pointed the finger and shifted the blame at one time or another.

Few people practice we/theyism on purpose. It's very likely that when you play the we/they card you do so subconsciously. You don't intend to subtly shift the blame, but you do so anyway, and for the most human of reasons: to make other people like you.

Let's say you and a coworker are in sales. The coworker asks you for some information about a discount, but the information you give them turns out to be incorrect. Instead of taking the blame yourself, you say, "I'm really sorry about that. I just forwarded you the information the Marketing Department sent me this morning. They should really double-check the information they send."

When Studer Group consults with organizations, we often discover that they are subject to we/they divisiveness. And what we find is that it really seems to come naturally to people. If it didn't, our seminar attendees wouldn't consistently label it the "number-one thing for my organization to stop doing." But they always do...and most people don't realize what a severe problem it is.

Fortunately, with focus and determination, any organization can stamp out we/theyism. Here's how:

Don't contribute to we/theyism yourself. The next time something goes wrong and you're tempted to blame someone else, stop and think: *How can I phrase this in a way that doesn't put others down—even subtly?* I'm not suggesting you take responsibility for an issue if it really isn't your fault; I'm simply suggesting that you phrase your communications in a neutral way. To go back to the sales example above, instead of shifting the blame to Marketing, you might say, "I'm sorry this information was wrong. Let me see if I can find the right numbers for you."

Manage up others when you can. Managing up simply means making an effort to position others—bosses, coworkers, departments, and even customers—in a positive light. Look for opportunities to do this. If some-one else is practicing we/theyism in your presence, you can counter with a positive (non-fake-sounding) state-ment: "I know the Marketing Department is really over-loaded right now. I'm not surprised they made a mistake! I find that when you let them know they sent the wrong information they fix it pretty quickly."

Send notes to your boss identifying employ-ees who deserve reward and recognition. Doing so helps them send thank-you notes, which are an impor-tant component of managing up. Remember, feel free to send thank-you notes to coworkers. When everyone at an organization feels appreciated, they are less likely to split the organization into a we/they culture.

Emphasize the importance of honest, open communication. If something is your fault, take the blame for it. If there is a problem between others, be your office mediator. Bring the necessary parties together and allow everyone to talk it out. Discourage people from pitting one group against another or allowing others to do so. And most importantly, always hold *yourself* to that standard.

Think about it like this: We/theyism is the antithe-sis of teamwork. It's people working against each other, rather than with each other. Even one person committing this sin can stop a department's or an organization's for-ward progress.

Of course, the opposite is also true. Just one person can break the we/they cycle and get everyone on the path to creating a positive, unified culture. Why not make it your goal to be that one person?

CHAPTER FOURTEEN:

DO THE RIGHT THING WHEN SOMEONE ASKS YOU TO KEEP IT CONFIDENTIAL

"I need to tell you something but you need to promise to keep it confidential."

"Please keep this just between us."

"I heard something today that I feel I have to tell you—but you can't tell anyone else."

We've all been in situations where these words are used. Someone wants to share a secret, and it can be very tempting to agree. Most of us naturally want to please others. Plus, it feels good to be a part of a team or inner circle.

Unfortunately, by agreeing to keep a secret before we know what the secret is, we may be putting ourselves, our leaders and coworkers, or the organization itself in jeopardy.

To be clear I am not talking about the vital confidentiality that comes with patient care or attorney/client privilege (for those readers who may work in medical or legal fields). Nor am I referring to matters best left to Human Resources. I am confident you can separate those legitimate confidentiality issues from the ones discussed in this chapter.

Let's imagine a coworker asks you to keep something confidential and you agree upfront. And then, suppose you hear something that's illegal, unethical, or violates the organization's values or policies—and the person makes it clear that they are *not* willing to go to higher-ups with this information.

At that point you'll have two choices: 1) either keep the promise and ultimately let the organization down, or 2) break the promise and go to the appropriate leader to share the information that you feel you have to share. Neither is a good place to be.

While I realize it's not possible to diagnose every person who needs to share secrets, confidential information, gossip, or sad news, I find most seem to have one thing in common: the need to create a bond with the receiver. Unfortunately, it's often an unhealthy bond that doesn't serve either of you well.

You may find there are certain people who routinely share issues and concerns with you. These conversations may center on how underappreciated the person feels. Or maybe they tell you they are interviewing for a job. Or maybe they want you to know the whole department is stressed out and everyone is overwhelmed.

When this happens, the person confiding in you may not ask you to do anything with the information. Sometimes they really just want to vent. (In very small doses venting may be harmless—but when it happens too often it will quickly turn into we/they divisiveness, gossip, and other destructive behaviors.)

Other times, the individual may be hoping you will go to someone with their concerns. Be careful that you are not being used. It's best to encourage others to carry their own message.

So how *should* you respond when someone asks you to keep something confidential? The best course of action is to be upfront and say: "While I appreciate the fact that you want to confide in me, I cannot promise to keep it a secret. It's just my policy not to make promises that, in good conscience, I can't keep. If you are having an issue with someone, my suggestion is to take it up with them."

Staying out of such situations may make you a little less popular with some. However, it will make you much more comfortable in your own skin and, in general, will make you a more desirable coworker. You'll be setting an example of mature behavior.

If the person blurts out the secret before you have a chance to stop them—or if you do respond as suggested above and they tell you anyway—there is still a chance to salvage the situation. You might ask, "What did Jeffrey (or whoever) say when you brought this up to him?"

Chances are, there will be silence. This is your opportunity to encourage the person to carry their own message. If you want, you can offer to coach them on how to do so. If they choose to take action, you will have helped them. For sure, you will have helped *you*.

One day I received a call from a leader. She told me that two of her coworkers had come to her one at a time to share how overworked and overstressed they were. She was very concerned about this. She went on to say that neither of these people reported to her. When I asked her why she thought they came to her, she said she did not know.

I had known this leader for some time. My impression was that she was a very caring person who was very concerned about others—good traits if used correctly. She also had a very good relationship with the CEO. I knew that while she did not report to him, she saw him often.

So I asked her, "In the past, when people have brought concerns to you, have you passed them along to the CEO?" She admitted that she had.

I told her I felt people gave her information because they wanted her to carry the message for them. And while in some exceptional situations this may be called for, it generally harms the organization. It's always better for people to develop their own skill sets.

A few weeks later I received a call from this leader. Another leader—one of the regulars—had stopped in to see her and brought out the same old concern: "I work so hard, I can't go on like this, no one appreciates me," and so on and so forth.

This time, the leader told me, she simply said, "I suggest you bring this issue to your supervisor." The coworker looked a bit startled and left.

She told me she felt liberated. She had finally realizec she did not have to be a messenger for others. She also said that, ultimately, she even felt more respected by the other person.

In every work situation most of us want to be liked, to be helpful, and to show empathy. These are good qualities. Unfortunately, they can be used incorrectly. When they are, they result in workplaces where relationships resemble adult/child interactions. Environments like these typically benefit only a few—and then for only a short time.

Used correctly, however, these same qualities help us to create healthy, mature work environments. These are the kinds of workplaces where people develop their skills, work together as a team, and create the best possible results for clients and customers.

CHAPTER FIFTEEN:

BUILD AN EMOTIONAL
BANK ACCOUNT

A workplace relationship is a lot like a marriage or a friendship: It's based on give and take. If you're a good spouse or a good friend, you probably make an effort to "give" most of the time: You try to make life easier and better for the other party. You're considerate and respectful, you clean up after yourself, you remember birthdays, you show up on time for lunch dates.

However, because no one is perfect, there will also be times you "take." Perhaps you snap at your spouse because you're tired. Or maybe you miss your friend's daughter's wedding because you accidentally scheduled your vacation at the same time.

Hopefully, because you've made an effort to do the right thing 90 percent of the time, your friend or spouse will be willing to forgive the other 10 percent. This is called building a strong emotional bank account: You make as many *deposits* as possible so that when you have to make a *withdrawal* the balance is still in your favor and the relationship doesn't crash.

The same principle holds true in the workplace. It's important to do everything you can, every day, to be the best employee and coworker you can be. Why? Because, inevitably, you will make a mistake and let the boss or a coworker down or you'll need to ask for a favor.

By working hard to build trusting, productive, and positive relationships with others in the workplace, you ensure there's enough emotional capital in the account to cover these metaphorical rainy days.

Basically, building a positive emotional bank account means doing what we can to make others in the workplace happy most of the time, in anticipation of those future times when we might, carelessly or unintentionally, let them down.

A few tips for building up your workplace emotional bank account...

Ask what you can do to improve. One way to make emotional bank account deposits is to reduce the risk you'll need to make an unexpected withdrawal. Ask people for honest feedback on how you can work better with them. Be sure to implement their suggestions and follow up to make sure the changes you make have affected them positively.

Go for "quick wins." Bring your cubicle mate a cup of their favorite coffee. Offer to take your coworkers' trash out when you're taking out yours. Congratulate them on a job well done. Recognize an important milestone like a birthday or anniversary. Cook a meal fo. a coworker's sick mother. Bring in a bag of cute clothing your kids have outgrown and give it to others who have younger children. These are all great ways to get quick wins, which translate into emotional bank account deposits.

Give credit when credit is due. When someone has a big win, make a big deal out of it. Congratulate the coworker personally, but also make sure everyone else knows they have done a great job. It will make them feel great, and that will make them feel great about you. Managing up the people you work with is a powerful way to make emotional bank account deposits—it provides a lot of bang for the buck.

Ask for their input. People like feeling valued. They like knowing that their opinions and thoughts truly matter. A great way to make deposits in coworkers' emotional bank accounts is to ask for their input on a problem you might be having. For example you might say, "Bob, I really admire how you handle your clients. I'm having a problem connecting with Client X. What do you recommend?" Showing Bob that you value his opinion will make him feel great, which will translate into positive feelings about you.

Be open and honest. Always tell the truth, avoid office politics and gossip, and never be two faced. You'll build credibility and trust, both of which are like having an accruing investment in an emotional bank account. When leaders and coworkers trust you, their good opinion of you will only continue to grow.

...And a few more for making withdrawals:

Apologize sincerely when you mess up. If you've made a mistake that is going to make someone's job a little harder—for example, if you've missed an important deadline or screwed up their client's order—before you do anything else, it's best to apologize. Acknowledge that your mistake is making their job more difficult and then offer to do whatever you can to make things right.

Don't ever point fingers or try to redirect the blame. Doing so will only mean a loss of credibility with coworkers, which will result in more emotional bank account withdrawals.

Show your gratitude. Whether you screwed up and need to be bailed out or had to miss work three days in a row because your child is sick, the end result is the same: Others had to step in and help you out. Be grateful. Follow up the help you've received with a thank-you note and make sure coworkers know that you know you couldn't have solved the problem or mistake without their help.

Follow up your withdrawal with a "pay back" gesture. If someone really went the extra mile to help you out of a jam, reciprocate. Take a tedious task off their hands or offer to edit the marketing report they're putting together. You might even want to give them a token of appreciation, like a gift card to a local spa or shop.

Ultimately, the emotional capital you invest in co-workers and leaders helps strengthen your relationships with them. You don't have to be a math person to see how the formula works. Your deliberate, daily deposits will all add up to the perception that you like them, value their contributions, and want them to succeed—and your occasional withdrawals will barely make a dent.

CHAPTER SIXTEEN:

STEP IN AND HELP WHEN THEY'RE OVERWHELMED

Y ou're settling into your morning, wondering what to tackle first on your to-do list when you hear it: the distressed moans and groans of an overwhelmed co-worker. They have a client presentation that will also be attended by all of the company's higher-ups and they've just hung up with *yet another* team member who needs to make significant changes to their part of the project.

Besides actually creating the presentation, you know this person is also responsible for getting the conference room in order and making sure everyone attending has an up-to-date agenda for the meeting. Since the mission is to land a new client and so many of the company's leaders will be in attendance, everything must be done to perfection. Unfortunately, given the revisions they've just been asked to make, it seems your coworker won't have time to get it all done.

What do you do? Do you stay focused on completing the not-quite-as-urgent tasks on your ever-growing to-do list? Do you offer a weak "Oh, I can't believe they keep making these last minute changes on you! But I'm sure you'll do great!" and *then* retreat back to your cubicle, out of the line of fire? Or do you bite the bullet, resign yourself to a more stressful work day, and offer your help?

The right thing to do, of course, is to lend a helping hand. Healthy, productive, thriving companies are made up of people who function as a team, not as a collection of individual "islands." It's when people have a sense of ownership for outcomes—in this case, that the meeting results in a new client—that they're willing to help out rather than exhibiting a "not my job" mentality.

If you have a sense of ownership, you realize that everyone is in the same boat. The company's goals are everyone's goals. When you contribute to the success of a coworker, you're also contributing to the company's overall success.

Unfortunately, for many, there seem to be more reasons *not* to help than there are *to* help. For example, there will certainly be times when you are so overwhelmed yourself that the thought of helping someone else with her overloaded to-do list doesn't even cross your mind. (Or, if the voice of conscience does speak up, you quickly silence it with the rationalization that no one ever steps up to help you.)

Or maybe, if you work in a siloed company, you have such a structured view of what does and doesn't fall onto your list of responsibilities that you feel uncomfortable stepping outside those boundaries to help someone in another department.

Finally, there's the fear of unknown repercussions. Sure, helping out might lead to a very successful presentation, but what if something goes wrong? *It's probably best if I just don't get involved,* you may conclude.

I would ask that you nix these misgivings and do the right thing. Rather than avoid coworkers in need, jump in to help them whenever you can. After all, you work together, so why not work *together?*

Rather than get bogged down in everything you can't do (or don't want to do!) for coworkers, focus on what you *can* do. Here are a few tips to get you started:

Realize that it doesn't have to be an "all or nothing" proposition. In a situation like the one I just described, you don't have to commit to being the coworker's right-hand man (or woman) for the rest of the day. But you could say something like, "I have an hour that I can spare. What can I help you with?" By lightening your coworker's load even by just a little, you'll be relieving some of their stress, and they can focus more energy on the all-important presentation.

Ask how you can be the most help. In tense situations, it's a natural instinct to jump in and just start doing things. However, without full working knowledge of the entire project, it would be unlikely that you could determine where your skills are most impactful. Asking the coworker how you can help allows them to figure out how to make the best use of your time. They know best what they can delegate. By making assumptions about how you can be helpful, you may only add to the already heightened stress level.

Once you are on board, don't second-guess or criticize. Sure, you can offer your suggestions, but don't add to someone's stress by constantly questioning the decisions they're making.

Don't participate in complaints about the boss or other coworkers. An overwhelmed coworker might try to relieve some of their stress by complaining about the higher-ups or her team members. Don't take the bait. Participating in such complaints will only prolong and feed their negative attitude. (Besides, it's a huge time waster!)

Encourage the coworker to stay focused on the tasks at hand. Instead of letting them get stuck in the negatives of the moment, remind them that it would be best to complete the project first and *then*—after the project is done—evaluate what changes might be made in the future to make projects like this one run more efficiently.

There will be many opportunities for you to lend a helping hand. New employees, for example, can become easily overwhelmed. Keep an eye out for them and if you see they are struggling, offer your assistance. (Just be careful not to become a "crutch" for the disorganized or un-motivated—there's a fine line between helping out and enabling.)

Having coworkers who appreciate you and think highly of you will make coming to work every day a pleasure—for everyone involved! And ideally, others will pay it forward the next time they see a coworker in need. These are the things harmonious work environments are made of!

CHAPTER SEVENTEEN:

Minimize Last-Minute Requests

H as this ever happened to you? It's 4:30 and you're putting the finishing touches on your monthly report. Things are clicking along pretty well, and you're feeling good about making the 5:00 deadline. All of a sudden, the phone rings. It's your co-worker Barbara asking you to take "just a quick look" at the newsletter that needs to go to print today.

A sinking feeling washes over you. (You've been down this road before with Barbara and you know what's coming.) Sure enough, as you scan the newsletter you see that several key points are missing. There is not enough time to fix this and meet the printing deadline. Also, even if you *could* get the needed changes made in time, you'll end up either missing your own deadline or delivering a (far) less-than-perfect finished product.

It's a dilemma. You don't want to drop the ball on your report—but you also don't want to be responsible for letting a substandard newsletter go out.

If last-minute requests happened only once in a while, it wouldn't be such a big deal. The problem comes when you find yourself dealing with chronic offenders. Whether you have to deal with one coworker who does this or a whole office full of them (sometimes it's a company culture issue), "last-minute requesters" tend to interrupt your train of thought and interfere with your results.

Fortunately, you can deal productively with people who've gotten into the habit of making last-minute requests and even "retrain" them. This will help you do your best work.

Helping coworkers who make last-minute requests change their work styles will make them more efficient and productive. This allows them to form better relationships with you and others.

Read on for a few tips on how to handle excessive last-minute requests:

Hold up the mirror. What kind of message are you sending? Often, a last-minute request feels excessive because you've already got 30 other things on your plate. At other times, let's say when you're having a slow day or when you've just tied up the loose ends on a couple of big projects, a last-minute request doesn't seem like that big of a deal. At those times, you might happily help a coworker with a last-minute request. As a result, the next time that person drops the ball on something they'll think, *Well, Sarah helped me last time this happened. I'll just ask her to do it.*

What you permit, you promote! Think about the precedent you've set with your past behavior. If you've taken on last-minute requests, done them, and never indicated that this is a problem for you, then you've reinforced that it's okay to do it.

Essentially, you trained them to think last-minute requests aren't a problem for you. If this is the case, then you'll have to start the groundwork for changing these behaviors with yourself and with your coworkers.

Put a request system in place. One way to prevent excessive last-minute requests is to put a process in place that gives people a protocol for making requests and lets them know how long certain tasks take. If you don't have the authority to put the process in place, you can ask your leader to help you. (They will appreciate your thinking it through and taking the initiative.)

At one organization where I worked, HR was being criticized for taking too long to approve new hires. When new hires were chosen, they would always have to go to HR for a drug screening, physical, and other checks. The managers doing the hiring would get upset because this process always took a couple of days and they needed the new hire in place right away. But the reality was that sometimes these managers were sitting on the hires until just a few days before they wanted them to start working. They thought HR wasn't being responsive to their needs, but HR thought these managers were coming to them at the last minute and putting a rush on a process that took time.

To solve the problem, we made a rule that as soon as a manager wanted to make a hire they were to send the person to HR, and HR would get back to them within 72 hours. By putting a process in place, we were able to put everyone on the same schedule so that no one was being rushed and no one felt like the ball was getting dropped. It helped everyone work together more harmoniously.

Educate people on how long a task takes. Often, when certain tasks don't ever fall under a person's job requirements, they may underestimate how long they take to complete. They may think something is very simple to do when in reality it is complex and involves a lot of steps or a lot of coordination between departments. For example, the Sales Department might want the Marketing Department to put a flier together for a conference that is happening in two days. What they might not realize is that in addition to writing the copy and designing the flier, there are also copyright and trademark issues to handle. Plus, printing will take a certain amount of time.

In my own experience, I've seen this dynamic inside hospitals. A patient might be waiting in the ER to hear about lab work. They might think the lab is dragging its feet on getting the results, when in reality, it can take two hours or more for certain tests to be done. We would explain this time issue to a patient by saying, "Sir (or Ma'am), your cultures will need to sit for a certain amount of time in order for us to get a valid result. I want you to know the process will take two hours." This would ease the patient's anxiety and allow them to have realistic expectations. They weren't just left in the waiting room, watching the clock, wondering, *What is taking so long?*

In your job when you receive a last-minute request, it's okay to say, "I am going to get this done as quickly as possible, but I want you to know that first we'll have to get Legal's approval, and then the printer will take at least one business day to print this number of fliers." Now the coworker knows what to expect, and that in the future they should allow more time for this kind of request.

Use collaborative problem solving. Once you've explained exactly what you have on your plate and exactly how long the task will take, and your coworker has told you exactly when they need the task completed, it's time to implement some collaborative problem solving. There might have to be some give and take between you and your coworker. For example, you might have to say, "In order to do it right, I can have it to you by the end of the day tomorrow. But in order to meet that deadline, I'll need your help doing this, this, and this."

Of course, it's possible that you'll already be working on a project that is more urgent than theirs. Let the coworker know when you'll be able to tackle their issue. Maybe you can tell them how to get their project started so that when you're free you can hit the ground running, or maybe you can suggest another coworker who will be able to help them.

When all is said and done and the dust is settled, ask to meet with the coworker. Make sure they understand that the task they brought to you will *always* take X amount of time. Explain that you're happy to help them on these projects, but that you will need X amount of notice to make sure you can complete the task by the deadline. Again, setting these parameters will help you both work better together.

Set consequences. Work with the boss to set consequences for all those who make last-minute requests. At one organization where I worked, every new employee had to go through an orientation program. They couldn't begin work without the orientation because it created a liability situation for the organization. Orientation sessions were regularly held every other Monday, and everyone knew this. Every now and then a department manager would have a new employee starting at the organization who hadn't yet completed orientation. We couldn't allow the new hire to start without doing orientation, so the manager would be upset. He'd say, "Well, then I'm going to have more overtime." We'd have to explain that because he waited until the last minute to make arrangements for the orientation, he missed out on allowing the new hire to start on the right date. We held tight on this every time it happened. It became a "what you permit, you promote" teaching opportunity. Eventually, the behavior stopped.

If you go back to the flier example from above, let's say the rule was that all marketing materials had to be approved internally before they could be used externally. The consequence might be that the flier is prohibited from being used until the right people have signed off on it. When you hold steady on these consequences, people will begin to change their behaviors.

Reward and recognize. Take a look at the employees who are always considerate of your schedule and do the proper planning to meet deadlines. Do you ever thank them for doing so? Or if this has been a problem with a coworker but they've made changes in their behavior to do better, have you recognized and rewarded this change? If not, then it's important that you start because behaviors that are recognized and rewarded get repeated.

For example, if a person who has in the past always given you last-minute requests doesn't this time, then after the task is complete go to them and say, "You know what, Mary (or Ralph or whomever), I want to tell you how much I appreciate you giving me plenty of notice on the Acme assignment. With everything going on right now the fact that you gave me ample lead time will make my work life better and will lead to a much better product for our client. Thank you."

Handling excessive last-minute requests essentially comes down to planning. Sure, on occasion, a situation will pop up where a last-minute task has to be completed, but by and large, issues can be avoided when the right amount of planning is done on the front end. Keep communication open with coworkers and work with the leaders at your organization to make sure that everyone is on the same page and knows the protocol for completing important projects.

Chapter Eighteen:

Mentor New Coworkers

After months of interviewing, the organization has *finally* made a decision. Everyone is satisfied that the right person has been selected, and your newest coworker is getting settled in. You've introduced yourself and done your "Welcome to the team!" greeting and now you can play a vital role in getting this new coworker off to a good start.

Studies consistently show that a significant percentage of employees who leave an organization do so within the first 90 to 120 days. In other words, those first few months are critical for new hires. (It's why Studer Group teaches leaders to hold 30- and 90-day one-on-one meetings with new hires—we find it reduces turnover by 66 percent.)

New employees do best when they are mentored from day one. They need someone to show them the ropes, answer questions, and tend to other concerns. That "someone" can be you. When coworkers do whatever they can to help new hires get settled in, it helps them become productive, thriving team members right away.

As a new employee's colleague and peer, you play an important role in their overall happiness. By mentoring the new employee, you can reduce the chances that they will become unhappy or ultimately decide to leave the organization—an outcome that negatively impacts everyone's morale and leads to a loss of time and money. Remember, it can cost the equivalent of a person's salary to replace them; for executives those costs can balloon to triple the salary, sometimes more.

Peer mentoring benefits both parties. The new coworker will enjoy having a helpful individual to go to when they need guidance or support. As the mentor, you'll have an increased sense of accomplishment and may even form a rewarding new friendship.

Plus, it's almost guaranteed that you'll learn something new in the process. Remember, the new employee is coming from a different company and bringing all of that institutional knowledge with them. When you work with them as a mentor, they're bound to make a suggestion or two that will help you work smarter and more efficiently.

Here are a few tips on how to mentor new employees, increase their job satisfaction, and help them develop into quality contributors at your organization:

If you can, get involved during the interviewing process. Ideally, building coworker/peer relationships with new hires begins during the interviewing phase. Work with the hiring managers at your organization to implement a peer interviewing process. When given the opportunity to interview a potential new hire, employees take a greater personal interest and sense of ownership in that person's success.

Ask key questions early on. Within the first one to two weeks of the new hire's start date, ask them to lunch. When you are one-on-one, find out more about what they enjoy doing outside the office and what their expectations are for the new position. Most importantly, ask what you can do to help them be successful. Find out how they like to work with and partner with coworkers, and make sure they know that if they ever need a helping hand, you're more than willing to help out.

Help the new hire integrate into the company culture. Ask the new hire if they would be okay with you providing advice when you see them doing something that doesn't serve them well—or not doing something that could benefit them in the company. For example, perhaps they aren't using the organization-wide standard for internal memos or maybe they're not quite following the dress code.

Make it clear to the new employee that while they don't have to follow your advice, you're happy to help in any way you can. You may even want to note any challenges you experienced when you first started with the company so they feel at ease discussing those issues with you.

Think of yourself as a role model. Telling the new employee what to do (and what not to do) isn't nearly as powerful as showing them by example. Make sure to follow all company policies and standards when you're around them. Model the work ethic, behavior standards, communication techniques, and other practices they'll need to follow in order to thrive at your organization. What you demonstrate is almost always more impactful than what you say.

Resist the temptation to "do it for them." It takes patience to talk a new employee through performing a task you've done hundreds of times. Sure, as an experienced staff member you can do it a lot faster. But allowing the new person to go through the steps themselves, no matter how long it takes or how many errors they make in the process, is the best way for them to learn.

Share all the information required to do the best job. It doesn't happen often, but occasionally I hear about a mentor giving a new employee the "short version" of how to do a job. Perhaps they withhold information because it seems faster to do the rest themselves, but sometimes it's because they want to protect their "expert" status. Make sure you're not subconsciously holding onto critical information because you fear not being the expert. Being good at what you do is great…helping others be good at what they do is even better!

Be a friend. The new coworker is almost certainly comparing their first few weeks of work with your company to their last week at their previous job. And what usually happens to an employee during the last week? Their former coworkers throw them a going-away party that includes a cake and a card signed by everyone with their well wishes and fond memories of how great it was working together.

They're wistfully comparing that experience to this new place where nobody knows them, no parties have been thrown, and very few well wishes have come their way. In fact, very few people actually call them by name. It doesn't take a rocket scientist to see that your company is getting the short end of an unfavorable comparison.

That's why it's a good idea to make an effort to not only show the new employee the ropes of the business side of the workplace, but to also make sure they're included socially. Draw them into water cooler conversations. Invite them to the weekly happy hour. And make sure they're clued-in on the fun side of the office, like casual Fridays or the free breakfast that is offered each Tuesday. Including them in these activities will go a long way in making them feel like part of the team.

Share tips. Naturally, the new coworker wants to be great in their new job. They want to provide great service to the company's customers and go the extra mile in any way they can. To help them do that, provide any insight you might have into how certain customers like to be handled and treated. If, for example, an on-the-go small business owner hates receiving calls and prefers to only be e-mailed, let the new employee know. Or if a customer is a huge fan of a local sports team or loves fishing, tell them about it so they can be sure to use that information as they build relationships with customers.

Set the new hire up for a successful relationship with the boss. Hopefully the boss is already working to form a great relationship with the new hire. However, you can help in this arena, too. Just as you've helped the new employee with customer relationships, provide some helpful hints regarding how best to handle the boss.

For example, explain how much the boss values receiving ideas from employees on how to improve the company and that they respond well to those who take the initiative to increase their level of responsibility. Or let the new employee know that the boss is usually at their best after their first cup of coffee in the morning! By showing the new hire the ropes, you can help them not only feel more comfortable but also form a relationship with the boss that allows them to truly thrive at the organization.

Remember, patience is a virtue! Anytime you start at a new organization, there is a lot to figure out. You have to learn how to navigate a completely different company culture, how to work with new people (in addition to learning who's who and who does what), and how to do your best work in this new environment.

What I'm getting at is that new hires have a lot on their plates. They are going to make mistakes, and certain things may have to be explained to them more than once. Be patient. Use mistakes as learning opportunities.

When an organization decides to tackle its problems with employee retention, it is making a commitment to excellence. I believe that a core focus on employee retention (rather than recruitment) serves organizations best.

What is important to remember is that you have an implied duty to the new hires at your organization.

Be their guide, be their sounding board, and provide them with the information they need to hit the ground running—straight toward long-term success at your organization.

The Joys of Being a "Buddy"

I find that mentoring is just as rewarding to the mentor as it is to the new employee. Anita Zefo, RD—currently director, food and nutrition services for Sutter Medical Center, Sacramento, CA—told me the following story:

Back when I worked as clinical and patient services manager at California Pacific Medical Center in San Francisco, I created a "buddy system" for new employees. Each time I hired a team member I asked one of my enthusiastic and savvy diet office staff to be their "buddy." Basically, they made themselves available for any question the new hire might have. Both mentors and new employees responded well to this system.

One day, I called one of our diet offices and got Gladys, a diet aide, on the phone. Just to give you a bit of back story, Gladys is from Hong Kong, and I had hired her for her first paying job in the U.S. Due to her inexperience, I had brought her on as a per diem diet aide and was thrilled to see her enthusiasm as she eventually worked her way up to a benefited position.

On this particular day, after Gladys and I exchanged greetings, she said, "Nita...why don't you ever ask me to be a buddy?" It was then that I discovered that, while I hurried around managing the day-to-day clinical aspects of our department, being asked to be a "buddy" had become something of a badge of honor. That was a great feeling! I assured Gladys that she would be the first person I called after hiring our next team member—and I fulfilled my promise.

There is no better win-win proposition than mentoring!

CHAPTER NINETEEN:

RESOLVE ISSUES ONE-ON-ONE WITH COWORKERS

C onsider an all-too-common scenario: Bob, your coworker, has inexplicably left you out of a meeting in which you would normally be included. You share your displeasure with the boss, who discusses it with a higher-up. The higher-up then spends time discussing the issue with you, your boss, and an HR rep. Each of these conversations takes time—time that is, frankly, mostly unproductive.

How could you have handled this instead? Well, before taking your complaints to the boss, you could have talked with Bob one-on-one. It's usually best for people to try to resolve issues amongst themselves before involving others. Doing so helps to build healthy, effective work relationships and helps save time and money spent when others are brought in to resolve conflicts that could have been settled quietly one-on-one. Plus, being willing to resolve problems on your own shows a good sense of ownership.

I find that when two people get together, they usually resolve issues pretty easily. For example, if you had spoken with Bob, you may have learned that he simply forgot to CC you on the e-mail about the meeting. By going to the boss, you would have created an HR problem based on a simple human error. Or you may have found that Bob didn't think you needed to be involved with the project discussed during that meeting.

The reality is that most of us do whatever we can to avoid confrontation. Perhaps you grew up in a home where serious issues were "buried" and thus you never learned how to disagree with others. Perhaps you're worried that the other person may retaliate. Or maybe you're just sensitive by nature and don't want to hurt someone's feelings.

The truth is, though, that all confrontation is not "bad." Without it, issues don't get resolved and they may even escalate. Whether we like it or not, confronting others is a necessary part of clear and productive communication. In order to be successful, we've got to be able to have adult conversations in the workplace. If there is a problem or an issue, it is best to discuss it directly with the other person or people involved. If a resolution can't be reached, then it's time to bring in the boss.

When resolving issues with coworkers, here are a few things to keep in mind:

If you feel you need it, get advice from a trusted peer or assistance from the employee assistance program. This may not be necessary but if after giving it a lot of thought you still have misgivings about confronting the coworker, it's better to be safe th. sorry.

Ask to meet privately. Send an e-mail asking to meet somewhere one-on-one or pull the coworker aside when the two of you are alone in the break room. The key is to meet somewhere secluded from the rest of the office—a conference room, for example—so that you can both speak freely, without being concerned about who else in the office is taking notice.

Use neutral language. Let's say you're resolving the meeting issue. Instead of saying, "What's your problem with me, Bob? Why did you purposely leave me out of yesterday's meeting?" you might want to take a gentler approach. Instead say, "Congratulations, I heard you are heading up the Acme project. You know, usually I take part in all of the project meetings for that client. Would you mind including me on the details for the next meeting?" By starting on a positive note, you open the door for Bob to be more receptive to what you have to say.

Apologize for your role in the conflict. If you're involved in a more serious conflict, for example an argument in a budget meeting, start the conversation off with an apology. Make amends for losing your temper and being unprofessional. While your coworker may not immediately warm to you, this sincere effort to clear the air won't go unnoticed, and you'll help defuse the situation enough for the conversation to take place.

Listen carefully. Remember, just because you are doing the confronting does not mean you're the only one who gets to speak their mind. This is not an opportunity

...ecture a coworker. It's an opportunity to hear that person out. *Actively listen* to what they're saying. You have to accept that their side of the story is just as valid as yours. By listening to what they have to say, you get one step closer to finding a compromise or solution.

Ask about solutions. While you're still in listening mode, ask the coworker what they think the right solution might be. You might be a-okay with the proposition they make, and if so, that's great. Accept it, and you can both move in a positive direction.

If you don't agree, offer a compromise that takes the coworker's solution into consideration while also adding a solution of your own. To return to the earlier example, you may have found out in your conversation with Bob that he didn't invite you to the meeting because you're in the Accounting Department and the Acme meeting was for brainstorming marketing campaign ideas. Perhaps Bob explained that he didn't want an accountant in the meeting because he didn't want his team to refrain from thinking big because they were concerned an idea might be shot down because of its expense.

If Bob says he'd rather not include you in any meetings, ask if it might be possible for you to be included in meetings once their ideas are more refined. Point out that in addition to keeping an eye on cost, you also have a lot to offer when it comes to finding cost-effective ways to make big ideas happen. Bob will probably find it difficult to turn down that offer.

If you continue to butt heads, call in the boss. If you can't come to a solution that meets everyone's approval and it's an issue that is going to affect productivity or customer service, then it's time to bring in the boss to help mediate. Don't live in silent scorn. The boss may run you both through the steps you've already taken, but it could be that their outside perspective is what's needed in order to find a solution.

Honest, open communication in the workplace is a must. Allowing conflicts to snowball isn't good for anyone involved. Don't be afraid to approach people when you have a work-related issue you need to discuss with them. You'll be saving yourself, the coworker, the boss, and the company as a whole valuable time and money.

Chapter Twenty:

Keep Meetings Productive

S ay the word "meeting" and too often you may be greeted with groans, sighs, and eye-rolls. (You may even let a "Here we go again!" slip out yourself.) And there's a good reason why: We all face heavy demands on our time and energy. We have more to do than we can handle, and the stakes are higher than they've ever been—so the last thing we have time for is another unproductive meeting.

It's not that "good" meetings don't exist. They do—and in a global economy where team members may be located halfway around the world they're more important than ever. It's just that too often we've come to expect meetings to be unfocused and unproductive.

That's too bad. When meetings are unproductive, *people* are unproductive. They get bored and zone out. They get off track and waste time. They walk away with no clarity on what needs to happen, who needs to do it, and when it needs to get done.

In fact, I find that what often happens is that some people leave meetings knowing what to do, while others don't. This harms alignment and can lead to inconsistent results throughout the organization.

On the other hand, when meetings are done right, they're a great communication tool. They get everyone on the same page. They ensure the right people are focused on the right goals and timelines. And they provide an opportunity for valuable brainstorming and collaboration. It's also important to note that when meetings are truly productive, a) they are shorter, and b) fewer of them are needed—further ensuring that everyone is able to focus as much of their time as possible on the tasks and projects that matter most.

Whether you're leading a meeting or just attending one, there is plenty you can do to make it a productive and positive experience for everyone involved. You'll make your own life easier, build goodwill among coworkers, and impress the boss with your efficiency and focus on making every minute count.

Here are a few things to keep in mind:

If you're LEADING a meeting:

Invite only the people who need to be there. Meetings work best when they are small. Think carefully about who really needs to be there. For example, could Kathy in Marketing be kept up-to-date by just reviewing the meeting minutes?

Send the agenda out in advance. Make sure it includes the date, time, and location as well as the points to be discussed and how long those discussions will last. This gives people a chance to think about what they will contribute.

Keep the meeting a reasonable length. You might be discussing the most important aspects of the company's upcoming goals, but if you're doing it at the end of a two-hour long meeting, your audience probably won't be taking in much of what you're saying.

Don't get caught up in minutiae. Meetings are best used to collectively set goals, brainstorm, and check on progress. They're not the right time to hammer out every little detail of a project. If Steve and John are asked to find a good venue for this year's client summit, the meeting where they receive that assignment is not the right time to start bouncing venue ideas back and forth. The two can do this research after the meeting and bring options for everyone to consider next time. Knowing what to put out to the group and what to take "off line" is a big part of successful meeting management.

Look for opportunities to inspire. When possible, mention something that is going well or remind people of the bigger purpose they're serving. Try to do this early on. It will put them in a good frame of mind and motivate them to do their best work during the meeting and afterward.

Carefully manage conflict. Some conflict can be good in a meeting. It gets people thinking and can lead to ideas that might not otherwise have been brought to light. But when conflict gets out of hand, the meeting will disintegrate. If a topic of discussion gets heated, you might need to end it for the moment with a promise that you'll reopen the discussion later. When you do reopen it, position it in a way that defuses the situation.

Keep people on track. One of the best ways to do so is to keep everyone engaged. Don't allow one person to dominate the discussion. When appropriate, go around the table to get feedback from everyone in attendance. If someone does seem to be getting off track, say, "Jessica, you've raised some very good points today. Let's see if anyone else wants to add to your ideas. Pete, would your department be able to execute Jessica's idea?"

Address deliverables and deadlines. Many of us get frustrated in meetings because we come away with a list of tasks to add to our ever-expanding to-do list, but aren't sure when they need to be completed or whether someone else might already be working on the same thing. When leading a meeting, don't just provide progress updates or recaps of what needs to be done. Assign deliverables and specific deadlines so everyone knows who is doing what and when.

End the meeting with a "stoplight" report. Take a few minutes at the end of every meeting to go around the table and review everyone's deliverables so that you can be certain everyone understands their goals to achieve before the next meeting. Assign every task or goal a color: Red means "Hold on this for now," green means "Full speed ahead," and yellow means "We'll think about this for a while longer."

Take good, detailed notes. Before every meeting, assign someone to take notes during the meeting. Make sure the notes are then distributed to everyone who attended and anyone who might not have attended but who will benefit from seeing what was discussed. Having documentation of what was discussed in the meeting will help keep people focused on the objectives they need to achieve.

Clarify what needs to be communicated to people after the meeting—when, how, and by whom. This will ensure that everyone on the team is on the same page. In most organizations, the decisions aren't the problem; the communication around them is. We spend all of our time and energy reaching decisions, then miss the opportunity to assure the best way to communicate those decisions. It's this last 10 percent that makes the previous 90 percent pay off.

Ask attendees to rate the meeting. Tell them, "Let's get any concerns out on the table." Ask them to rate the meeting with a number between one and five. If it's a five, ask them what made it a five. If it's anything lower, ask them what might have been done differently to make it a five.

If you're ATTENDING a meeting:

When you attend a meeting, you are not just a bystander. You can exert a lot of influence on the meeting's effectiveness. Here are a few tips:

If necessary, lead the leader. When meetings at your organization are time-consuming and unproductive, take ownership. That doesn't mean making a power move and taking over the meeting yourself. Instead, you might pull the meeting leader aside and give them an article on how to run a good meeting. You might say, "I am sure running all those meetings can be stressful, and I know how committed you are to running good meetings. I saw this and thought you might be interested."

Or if the person running the meetings repeatedly comes without an agenda, pull them aside and say, "I know you're committed to communicating with us effectively, and I know running these meetings is difficult, but one thing that I think would help keep us all on track is a meeting agenda." You might then offer to show them a sample of an agenda or even help them put one together before the next meeting. I find that when you compliment a behavior before it happens, you'll often see that it starts occurring. So by telling the leader that you know how strongly they feel about running good meetings, you'll be setting the stage for them to do exactly that.

Do your part to keep everyone on topic. Another way to take ownership is by subtly helping the meeting leader keep everyone on track. If an agenda item has trailed off into a conversation about something else, you can be a leading peer and help get the meeting back on track. Politely interrupt the conversation and say, "I think this is a great discussion, but I think it's really important that we have enough time to discuss the next item on the agenda." Or, "This conversation is really interesting, but I've been looking forward to hearing what everyone thinks about this next agenda item." Often, giving a nice subtle tip will be all that is necessary to bring people back to the agenda.

Get some talking points ready. Read the meeting agenda ahead of time and think about where you can contribute. Be prepared with talking points that pertain to items that involve you. Remember, when you sit in silence you seem unengaged—you may be paying close attention but no one will be able to tell.

Arrive early. This will give you a chance to get seated and take another look at the meeting agenda so that you can organize your thoughts and do some last-minute preparations. The same applies if you're attending the meeting virtually—always call in or sign on promptly.

Take your own notes. There will probably be an official note-taker at the meeting, but it's still a good idea for you to take notes on the items that pertain directly to you. What if the person in charge of capturing what happens in the meeting does a less than thorough job or leaves out some critical detail?

Don't check your e-mail, text, or work on anything unrelated to the meeting agenda. Not only will tapping away at electronic devices keep you from engaging fully in the meeting, it's disrespectful to others. Just don't do it.

Don't contribute too much or too little. Don't monopolize the conversation. If you're a big talker, make sure what you say is productive and helps keep the meeting moving forward. And if you normally like to hide in the shadows, speak up. (This is where you'll be glad you prepared your talking points ahead of time.) You may even make checkmarks each time you talk. This will help you assess "Do I talk too much or do I not talk enough?"

Double-check your responsibilities. Before you leave the meeting, make sure you understand *exactly* what you're supposed to do, when it needs to be delivered, and how. If you're not sure, ask for clarification.

Follow up. After the meeting, send a follow-up e-mail detailing what you're going to do and when you will be delivering it. This will provide the meeting leader one more chance to clarify any tasks that you might have misunderstood. And if the boss isn't the team leader, make sure to copy them so they'll know what you're doing, too.

Reward and recognize leaders who run good meetings. If there's any skill today's leader needs, it's the ability to make sure everyone uses their time effectively. So when a leader is doing a great job running meetings, encourage them by rewarding and recognizing their efforts or improvements. For example, if a leader who hadn't been providing an agenda starts taking the time to do so and is working hard to keep everyone on topic, pull them aside and say, "I think I speak for everyone when I say that having those agendas has really helped. And thanks for keeping excess conversations to a minimum so that we can all make the meetings time well spent." Or, "Thank you for the follow up e-mail you sent after the meeting. It really helps me to see everything I am responsible for in writing."

How you conduct yourself in meetings goes a long way toward shaping your brand. It's probably the time you're most visible to leaders and coworkers. This is especially true if you work virtually or participate on virtual teams, because meetings are the only times most coworkers get to interact with you.

Make the most of meetings. Not only will leading and participating in them the right way help you do your own job better, it can help make a positive impact on the people you work with and the organization itself.

CHAPTER TWENTY-ONE:

Say You Are Sorry When You Are Wrong

"A stiff apology is a second insult...The injured party does not want to be compensated because he has been wronged; he wants to be healed because he has been hurt."
—Gilbert K. Chesterton

We all mess up from time to time. We miss an important deadline. We interrupt a coworker on an important phone call. We show up late for a critical meeting. We get caught in the act of gossiping about someone. There is literally no end to the list of mistakes we can make, balls we can drop, and ways we can hurt others' feelings.

But these mistakes aren't what define us. It's how we act after the fact that determines our character as employees and coworkers. If we're the stubborn type who can never admit to making a mistake, people will trust and respect us less. But when we are willing to say we're sorry, they'll be more willing to forgive us for our mistake.

Both contrition and forgiveness are essential to healthy relationships. A sincere, heartfelt apology expresses the former and almost always results in the latter. That's what makes it such a valuable tool for workplace communication.

Apologizing shows one's vulnerability, and vulnerability is a powerful trait. People fear they'll be rejected if they show weakness or admit that they failed. The opposite is true. It actually makes people like us. It shows we're human, just like them.

Also, when we admit we're wrong, others are more likely to admit *they're* wrong. It sets a healthy precedent and creates openness and authenticity.

Here are a few tips to keep in mind when you have to bite the bullet and apologize:

Say you're sorry right away. First of all, apologizing quickly defuses anger. Waiting causes anger to escalate. Soon a problem that could have been defused with a simple "I'm sorry" requires a lot more attention… and the relationship could suffer permanent damage.

Plus the longer you wait, the less believable you'll be. Ever notice how politicians and celebrities "apologize" only *after* they're caught—even if the offense happened months or even years ago? By that time, the apology doesn't ring true. We all know they're just apologizing because they got caught. Don't follow in their footsteps. Come clean as soon as possible.

Apologize face-to-face, or at least on the phone. This is one time e-mail won't cut it. Apologizing via e-mail might cause the person to think you aren't sincere or just didn't care enough to meet with them one-on-one. Apologizing face-to-face or by phone will allow them to hear and/or see that you are sincere and that you want to do whatever you can to mend the relationship.

Mean it. An insincere apology is worse than no apology. Really think about your misdeed from the other person's perspective before you apologize. This will most likely help you apologize sincerely.

And yes, there may be occasions you truly don't feel that you were in the wrong with something you said or did, but your words or actions hurt the other person—and you do regret *that*. In those cases a simple "I'm sorry I hurt you" allows you to apologize without admitting wrongdoing.

Be specific about the problems your mistake has caused. It's important to be sincere in your apology, and a generic "I'm sorry" may seem meaningless. You need to show that you know what you should be sorry about. So use detail when making your apology. For example, you might say, "By getting the sales report to you three days late, I know I made it almost impossible for you to get your part done on time. I know you had to work late on Friday to meet your deadline, and I'm so sorry I caused you so much stress."

Don't make excuses. It detracts from the power of the apology when you say, "I'm sorry, but here's why it happened..." and then go into a laundry list of excuses.

Leave the "buts" out of your apology. It's fine to explain why the error was made, but don't dwell on that part.

Allow people to be angry. Be quiet and listen to what the person has to say. You have to humbly accept that someone you've wronged has the right to be angry at you. Remember, if you don't "allow" them to be angry, you probably aren't very sorry after all.

Make amends. Do what you can to "fix" your mistake and make it right. This might require you to go the extra mile for quite some time with the coworker you've wronged, but it will be worth it to mend that relationship.

While you should always apologize, don't beat yourself up too much when you make mistakes, especially those mistakes that couldn't have been prevented. Remember, mistakes are stepping stones on the path to excellence. As long as you learn from them and don't repeat them, they are valuable partners on that journey.

SECTION THREE:

WORKING BEST WITH YOUR CUSTOMERS

CHAPTER TWENTY-TWO:

ALWAYS, ALWAYS MANAGE UP THE COMPANY

Winning customers and keeping them happy is difficult. That means everyone needs to be engaged in building the organization's brand, and it needs to happen with every customer interaction. It used to be that this level of dedication and engagement was a "nice to have." Now, it's a "must have."

Managing up the company is all our jobs.

You've seen managing up before. When you go to a nice restaurant, the server doesn't just point to a blackboard with the daily specials. Instead, they say, "I tried today's pasta special before my shift and it's fabulous." Or when it is time for dessert, she says, "Gee, I don't know if you know this, but our executive chef was trained in New Orleans at Commander's Palace. That's who is creating our desserts today."

That's managing up. It's very powerful. When the server positions the restaurant, the food, and the chef in a positive light, you order with great anticipation. You probably enjoy it more than you would have if the server had described it in a neutral way. And you walk away feeling good about your decision to visit that particular restaurant.

Managing up works in any industry. In an upscale clothing store it's when the salesperson says, "We've really got some great new summer styles this season. Our buyer is fantastic—he is from Milan and has that famous Italian eye for fashion." In a hospital it's when the nurse says, "Dr. Harris has been a gastroenterologist for 20 years. He does this procedure hundreds of times a year. His patients love him and I know you will, too."

It will work for your organization, too. Essentially, it means saying positive things about the company's products and services, others in the organization, and of course the organization itself. At Studer Group, we help clients learn how key words at key times work so that managing up gets hardwired into a company's culture—but as an individual you can do this on your own.

Managing up the company and its offerings works on several levels:

- Most obviously, it helps you see the product or service you're trying to sell.
- It alleviates customer anxiety. Your customer wants to know that doing business with you is a good decision. When you say great things about your company and your coworkers, you make them feel that they are in the right place with the right company.

- It helps the customer form a positive opinion of the company. When you say "This is the best accounting firm/dentist office/car parts manufacturer/ad agency in the business" people tend to believe it more than if you just let the product or service represent the company. (Remember the restaurant example?)

All of this, of course, is good for you. What you're trying to do (depending on your job, of course) is make the sale or keep the customer happy—and hopefully create a return or long-term customer.

Managing up also makes your job easier because a happy customer is a lot more pleasant to work with. The rave reviews you'll get from customers will surely impress the boss. Coworkers, too, will appreciate the positive things you say about them.

Finally, managing up is a powerful form of "self-talk." You're not just selling the customer on the company; you're selling yourself on it. You're reminding yourself why you like your job, and that positive attitude will help you stay engaged and dedicated.

If you're not used to doing it managing up can take some getting used to. Here are a few tips to get you started:

Be authentic. If you aren't sincere when you are managing up the company, the customer will see right through you. Most people can sense "fakeness" from a mile away. Find something positive you really believe in to say about the product or a coworker.

If all else fails you might fall back on positive things other customers have said about your company. For example: "We have one customer who's a caterer and shops exclusively in our Kitchenware Department. She says the cookware we sell is the best in town and even though it may cost a little more the lifetime guarantee makes it money well spent."

"Narrate" the sales process or the service provided. When Studer Group works with healthcare organizations, we teach people to explain what they're doing as they're doing it. When they understand why a nurse is doing what they're doing, they perceive their care as far better than if the nurse had just silently performed the procedures.

The same is true for your job. When you explain why you structured your contract the way you did, or why you have to do a credit check or why a product has a particular feature, people will think more highly of your company. People always want to know *why*. When they don't, they assume the worst.

Don't ever make a "we/they" statement to a customer. This is especially an issue if a customer is disgruntled or complaining. You might think you're building a rapport by agreeing with the customer that another department is disorganized or that another employee has a bad attitude—with the implication being "But don't worry; *I'll* take care of you!"— but really all you're doing is further hurting the company. The customer thinks, *They're a nice employee, but I'm never doing business here again.*

Don't "manage down" the competition. Yes, it can be tempting to "bash" your company's competitors but it's usually best to resist. It comes across as unprofessional, plus, you never know who you're talking to—what if their spouse or sister or best friend works for the company you're badmouthing? Take the high road and you won't regret it.

Manage up the company when you're off the clock, too. When you're out in the community— especially if you're wearing a nametag or uniform but even if you're not—talk positively about who you work with and where you work. You're a representative of the company 24/7. (And thanks to social media that's literally true. Facebook never sleeps—and what you post there lives in cyberspace forever.) People hear what you say off the clock and take it to heart. It certainly influences their thoughts about the company and you.

When I lived in a town where a major carmaker was located, I used to hear employees jokingly say, "Don't ever buy a car that was built on a Friday or Monday because on Fridays we are getting ready for the weekend and on Mondays we are just coming back from the weekend." Now, I know they were joking, but still it certainly didn't make me want to run over to that company's dealership and buy a car. Watch what you say off the clock, and when you know you have people's ears, deliberately manage up the company.

In the end, the power of this technique comes from one central truth: People respond to positivity. They like positive people and they like hearing positive things about what they're spending their hard-earned money on. Positivity smoothes the sales process and keeps customers coming back to your organization again and again.

By mastering the art of managing up, you become an ambassador of positivity—and you and your entire organization will reap the benefits.

CHAPTER TWENTY-THREE:

PRACTICE THE AIDET APPROACH TO SERVICE

You probably know most aspects of your job and what your company does like the back of your hand. You know how long certain processes take. You know what all the steps are. And you know where to expect the occasional problem. But do you adequately communicate this knowledge to customers?

If you're a tailor, do you let the customer know exactly how long it will take for you to hem his pants? Or if you're a plumber, do you explain the process you'll be using to find the client's leak and how long you expect it to take? For too many, the answer is no. When we do something every day we may assume our customers are familiar with the fundamentals and know what to expect. They aren't. They don't.

We may think, for instance, *Well, it's no big deal. I'll just call the customer when their pants are ready.* Or, *I'm the one doing the plumbing so why do they need to know every step of the process?* Here's the short answer: Information reduces anxiety—

and a less anxious customer is an easier-to-deal-with, more satisfied, and ultimately more loyal customer.

I find that when people don't know what to expect, they invariably expect the worst. It's just one of those truths of human nature I've seen over and over in my decades of working with people all over the country. So when you narrate the transaction or service—that is, explain exactly how things are going to unfold and on what timetable—you set their mind at ease.

Just consider how you feel when you take your car into the shop because it's making an unsettling noise. What would make you feel better? Having the mechanic say, a) "We'll take a look at it when we can and let you know if we can find anything," or, b) "I'll be able to take a look at it in two hours. We'll run a diagnostics test to find out where the problem is. I'll give you a call at 3:00 p.m. to let you know where we are. At that point I'll give you an estimate and we can decide where to go from there."

Most people probably agree that Option B sounds better, right? No, you don't know any more about what's wrong with your car than you might have with the first mechanic, but you like this one better. Specifically, you trust them more. You feel better about leaving your car in their capable hands and they've given you a great first impression of the shop they work for—one that you'll remember the next time you need a car repair.

When we at Studer Group work with healthcare organizations we help them implement a process called AIDET^{SM}—whose letters stand for *A*cknowledge, *I*ntroduce, *D*uration, *E*xplanation, and *T*hank you—that's designed to put nervous patients at ease. It has proven its value over and over.

Though AIDET was initially developed for use in healthcare, I have found that it can be used successfully in customer interactions in any industry. If you're interacting with a customer for the first time, or working with an existing customer in a new capacity, AIDET can help you get the relationship off on the right foot.

Here's how it works:

A—Acknowledge. Say hello and greet the customer.

I—Introduce. Introduce yourself, your skill set, your professional certification, and your training. This builds your credibility, and the customer's confidence, right up-front.

D—Duration. Describe what you're going to do for the customer, how long each step will take, and so forth. This alleviates uncertainty and makes the customer feel more comfortable.

E—Explanation. Go into detail about important aspects of what you're doing. Remember, an educated customer is a happy customer.

T—Thank you. Quite simply, thank the customer for choosing your spa...or hair salon...or car detailing service. "Thank you" goes a long way.

Organizations and individuals that practice AIDET tend to stand out from the crowd. People remember them. For instance, my son Quin told me about a great experience he had with a company that might as well have been following the AIDET script. He hired Badger Basement Systems to do some repairs and waterproofing in his home and was delighted by the level of service they provided.

Specifically, the Badger Basement guy:

A—Greeted Quin in a friendly and professional manner.

I—Not only introduced himself and his assistants, but actually handed Quin résumés for each person who would be working on the basement.

D—Explained exactly how long the process would take. As any homeowner knows, having contract work done is very disruptive. Knowing the duration of the process, upfront, helped Quin mentally prepare himself for the chaos.

E—Explained the procedures to be done, in detail. In fact, he directed Quin to the company's highly educational website, which has a "learning center" link that delves into reasons basements leak and outlines all the options for repair.

T—Concluded the service with a sincere *thank you*.

Practice using AIDET in customer interactions until the technique becomes second nature. Then, you can teach it to others inside the organization. As I've said throughout this book, there is no reason to wait for a leader to implement a best practice—test it out yourself and then share the results with the boss and coworkers.

Just make this the message you hammer home over and over: AIDET is a great way to make customers, new and old, immediately feel at ease. When customers feel at ease they trust you. And they'll keep coming back to the companies they trust.

Chapter Twenty-Four:

Practice Good
Handovers

T hink about your favorite "service" person. It may
be the mechanic who works on your car or the
woman at the dry cleaner you entrust your favorite gar-
ments to or the pharmacist who fills your prescriptions.
Now imagine that you go for an appointment or show
up at the store only to find that the person you're used
to isn't there—and that you'll be dealing with someone
entirely new.

Here's another variation on the same theme: You're
in the hospital following a minor procedure and you've
gotten to really like the awesome nurse who's taking care
of you. Just as bedtime rolls around, lo and behold another nurse takes over…and you're not at all sure you're
comfortable with this change.

Most people in business call the event when Employee
A turns over care of a customer to Employee B a "handoff." Personally, I prefer the term "handover." (To me,
"handoff" seems to imply that an employee is completely

done with the customer, when often, that isn't the case at all.)

Handovers aren't unusual. We've all experienced them. But admit it—when a handover happens, you feel a twinge of anxiety. You probably *don't* think, *Oh good, a new employee! I'll bet they're even better than the one I usually see!*

In fact, you most likely expect the worst.

No doubt about it: People like familiarity. We're happier inside our comfort zones. So it's no wonder customer handovers are so tricky for companies.

It's just a fact that when one person is in charge of a particular customer things go more smoothly. That person's "institutional memory" of the customer's account and their likes and dislikes is incredibly powerful. That's why customer handovers are "moments of truth" for any organization.

Handovers may be where mistakes happen, balls get dropped, and misunderstandings reveal themselves...or they may be where an organization's true excellence and devotion to service shine through.

In today's world it's less and less likely that the same person will handle every customer interaction. Business happens across different geographic locations, different time zones, even different continents. Combine that with the "24/7" expectations of today's customers and there's no way around it—handovers are the norm.

That's why it's up to everyone to make sure they happen smoothly. Ensuring that customers experience good handovers goes a long way toward countering knee-jerk negativity and low expectations.

Remember, to customers, everyone they come into contact with is "the company." In their minds, you aren't Mary or Julio or Alexander. You're the face of the company. No matter how much a customer likes you, if they don't like the person who helps them after you, they process that as not liking the company as a whole. And that's the biggest *why* I can think of for making sure handovers happen as smoothly as possible.

A big part of good handovers involves proactively passing along information that will help the next person best serve the customer. This is actually a process that starts long before it's time for the handover. A few suggestions:

Pay attention to the customer's *what*. Everyone has a *what*. Your customers' *whats* will vary but they're the one or two things that must happen in order for them to be happy with your company. One customer's *what* might be to handle all communication over the phone rather than by e-mail. Another customer's *what* might be always receiving updates about their account on Tuesday.

Whatever the *what* is for a customer, paying attention and responding to it is not only a cornerstone of great service, it's a key element in handovers. When you hand over the customer to another employee, you emphasize the importance of always meeting that *what*. (Learn more about this topic in Chapter 25—"Know the Customer's *What*.")

Keep good records of customer preferences. You probably know your customers' likes, dislikes, and other nuances pretty well. (Yes, this includes their respective *whats* but also goes beyond them.) For example, one of your biggest customers might hate being called on their cell phone after 5:30 p.m. because they don't want their family time interrupted. By keeping detailed and updated records of these preferences, you'll be prepared to share that vital info with the next customer service person to prevent them from inadvertently doing something the customer doesn't like.

If possible, do handovers in the presence of the customer. This is a technique commonly used in healthcare. (If you've ever been in the hospital, you may have noticed that the outgoing nurse shares all the pertinent information about you with the oncoming nurse at your bedside.) The practice works well in any industry.

Conducting handovers in the customer's presence (in person or on the phone) has many benefits.

1. It allows the employee the customer is already comfortable with (Employee A, also known as you) to introduce the new one (Employee B).

2. By telling the customer's story to Employee B, you keep them from having to do it themselves. (Customers get frustrated when they have to explain the same thing over and over again.)

3. When you share information in front of the customer, you give them the opportunity to jump in and correct you if you happen to say the wrong thing.

4. It also allows them to ask questions on the spot and for you to hear Employee B's answer. This allows you to speak up if your coworker misunderstands something or to set them on the right path later if you hear them say something you know won't sit well with that customer.

Manage up the employee you're handing the customer over to. Handovers are also perfect occasions to manage up coworkers. Any time you pass a customer on to another department or another team member, you can view it as an excellent opportunity for managing up, which will go a long way toward alleviating the customer's anxiety.

For example, my daughter's battery is running out and the car won't start. I jump the battery and drive the car to Whibb's Automotive. The front-desk person, Bob, listens to my problem and says, "Mr. Studer, we're sending your car to Bay 7. Steve is our mechanic today. He will check out both your battery and your alternator. I want you to know that Steve is a certified mechanic. In fact, when it comes to fixing the alternator, Steve is one of the very best people we have in this entire garage."

Now, I'm thanking Bob for giving me to Steve, and I'm already genuinely happy that Steve's fixing my car. See the power of managing up? Obviously, you don't want to tell a customer something that's not true. But I find that most of the time we do work with talented people who know what they're talking about—we just don't think to relay that to customers.

If a customer is already upset, think twice about handing them over to someone else. When dealing with an already angry customer, it might be better to handle the rest of his transaction yourself, even if it's outside your job description. Passing them off to a coworker, even if that is usually how things are done, will probably upset them even more and may lead to them leaving the company altogether. By continuing to work with the customer, you can build a rapport and hopefully gain their trust.

If you are Employee B in the handover, make sure to ask Employee A for information on how to please the customer. The coworker may not always volunteer the information so take the initiative and ask. If they can't think of anything, you might want to ask some probing questions. For example, you might want to find out the customer's preferred method of communication, whether they like to be called by their first name or addressed more formally, etc. These are the little things Employee A might take for granted and forget to convey to you. It always helps to ask.

Of all the organizations I've worked with over the years, I've found that most have excellent employees in every department. Unfortunately, if the transition from one department to another isn't handled properly, customers never realize it. One bad handover experience can ruin their impression of an entire company.

You as an individual can go a long way toward changing this reality. Putting a little extra effort into handovers will help you become a more valued employee, will set the next employee up for success, will make the customer happy, and will strengthen the organization as a whole.

CHAPTER TWENTY-FIVE:

KNOW THE CUSTOMER'S *WHAT*

These days, you have to do more than provide great service to win over a customer and keep them coming back. You have to create the right experience *for them*. Every customer is different, so every experience will be (at least a little) different.

To give the kind of specialized, tailored attention that earns loyalty in an age of extreme consumer skepticism and endless choices, it's important to know what really matters to each person who buys your products or services. You have to know and constantly deliver on the customer's *what*—meaning what matters most to that particular person.

Maybe Customer A likes tons and tons of information before they make a decision, and Customer B wants you to only hit the high spots—they're too busy or impatient to sift through thousands of pages. Remember, only the customer knows what good service looks like *to them*.

It's up to you to find out what that is and to meet that standard every time.

When you take service to a personal level and strive to meet individual customer needs, it makes people feel special and lets them know you care about what matters to them. They know you aren't just following a standard customer service protocol because you've just given them their coffee exactly the way they like it while they wait or you've packaged their order exactly to their specifications. You've satisfied their *what*.

When you recognize and deliver on a customer's *what*, you make a big difference in how people perceive the company. You also build up a healthy emotional bank account, which means that if you ever do drop the ball or disappoint the customer, they will probably forgive you. It won't be a deal breaker.

This kind of personal service smoothes your relationship with customers and earns you lots of kudos—which makes you happy and also pleases the boss.

Read on for a few tips that will help you figure out your customers' *whats* and satisfy them every time.

Ask. Don't guess. Question the customer to make sure you really know what their *what* is and aren't just guessing. If you're talking to a new customer, you'll want to ask at the beginning of the very first interaction: "John (or Francine or whomever), I want to be mindful of your time today, so what expectations do you have for our call?" This will help you assess the customer's *what* and will let them know upfront that you truly want feedback.

Whatever you do, don't try to guess the customer's *what*. A lady would take her vehicle to a car wash near her office. She originally liked the car wash because they moved her car through very quickly and did a great job. One day, though, their service focus seemed to switch from speed to customer pampering. The manager would greet her at the door, give her coffee and something to read—but her car took much longer to get cleaned.

Then on what might easily have been her last visit, the manager asked her how she liked the new service. She took the opportunity to tell him that she had actually valued their speedy (but still good) service. She did *not* care about the plush new waiting area or the gourmet coffee. Ultimately, the car wash switched back to the kind of customer service its busy customers—at least that particular customer—appreciated.

Excellent customer service is subjective. Only the customer knows the answer. If you don't ask, you'll never know what their *what* really is. All the guessing in the world is worthless compared with the simple yet powerful act of getting the customer to tell you what they *really* want from you.

Don't let your own judgments/prejudices get in the way. You may not think it's reasonable for a customer to want you to call and go over every detail of their order after they've placed it or to require that you use a special kind of fertilizer on their yard or that you arrange their hotel room in a very specific way. But it doesn't matter. The customer, as they say, is always right. And their *what* is their *what*. It's up to you to find a way to provide the level of service that will satisfy that *what* and make them happy.

Keep a record of customer preferences. Keeping up with all of your customers' *whats* can be a challenge, so it's a good idea to have a system in place that helps you remember them. Customer preference cards are perfect for this. (Our hospital clients create them for both patients and physicians and they work wonderfully.) It doesn't *have* to be a card, of course—notebooks, files, and electronic documents may work better for you. What's important is that you keep some sort of record of what matters most to customers.

Depending on the business you're in, customer essentials might include the time of day they prefer to be called, the fact that they hate e-mail and never check theirs, that they don't want a certain kind of wax used on their car, etc. Keeping these records makes providing individualized service for your customers a little easier. Not only will they help you remember what the customer's *what* is, they'll help you ensure that handoffs go smoothly and that others in the company know what to do or say when dealing with that customer—and perhaps even more important, what *not* to.

Narrate the service you provide and work the customer's *what* into your words. For example, if you're a daycare teacher addressing a concerned parent, you might say: "I know it's really important to you that Carly gets a good nap because you have such a long commute in the mornings. Therefore, I am letting her sleep

20 minutes longer than the other kids. I just let her sleep while they're having free playtime."

This does two things: 1) It lets the parent know you know what's important to her and are making a conscious effort to meet that need, and 2) It gives her a chance to correct you if you assumed wrong. For example, it gives her an opening for saying, "Actually, she's started sleeping in the car in the mornings and it works out okay. I'd rather she got to spend that time socializing with the other kids."

Realize the *what* may change over time. Let's say you work in an upscale clothing store. Maybe when the economy was better and disposable incomes were flowing your customer Ellen wanted you to call her practically every time a "hot" (trendy) item came out. But with the economy slow down her priorities have shifted—now she wants you to make her aware of classic fashions that will stand the test of time.

It's perfectly normal for your customers' *whats* to change as their life situations change. Pay close attention to what they do and say and follow up with them frequently to make sure you are providing the kind of service they need.

Finally, if for some reason you can't accommodate the *what*, let the customer know why. See if you can make it up to them some other way. Maybe what they want is against the law (for instance, if you're a homebuilder and they request something that's against local ordinances). Or maybe because of the bad economy you've had to discontinue a service that you used to offer. Either way, let the customer know why you can't provide what they want—most people are reasonable when they understand there's a good reason for your "no."

Then, make sure you do what you can to make the customer happy. If you're the homebuilder, you can offer a modification that still satisfies what they want, but is also up to code. Or if you've discontinued a customer's favorite service, you can refer them to someone else or offer a discount on a service that you think they might also like.

I find that while most organizations sincerely want to provide the kind of individualized service I've described here, many just never figure it out. That's good news for you. It makes your organization stand out from the competition. And it makes customers far less likely to leave you. They know they can't get this kind of service just anywhere…and you get to feel a tremendous sense of pride in making a difference in their lives.

CHAPTER TWENTY-SIX:

PUT YOURSELF IN THE CUSTOMER'S SHOES

I t is natural to view the work we do through "company" eyes. We see our operations, the products and services we provide, and our interactions with customers from *our* perspective. This is normal and, to a certain degree, inevitable—after all, we're immersed in our world 40 hours a week, 52 weeks a year, and we just get used to thinking about things a certain way.

What it's all too easy to forget is that life looks a lot different from the customer's point of view. That's why it's important to put yourself in their shoes from time to time.

Companies that do this are able to truly serve their customers' needs (rather than their own perception of what those needs should be). Individual employees who do this can connect with their customers in meaningful ways that keep them satisfied and position the organization in a positive light.

In today's global marketplace, customers have endless choices. They can buy from companies almost anywhere in the world at anytime with relative ease. And with the struggling economy and money being tight, they're being more selective about where they spend their money— and they have high expectations when they do spend it.

If their needs are not being met, they might very quickly decide to go with a competitor. Once a customer drops you, it can be very difficult to win them back.

Companies need to be absolutely certain they're looking at what they do and say through the customer's lens. As an employee, educate customers on why you're doing what you're doing, alleviate any anxiety they may feel, and go the proverbial "extra mile" to please them.

When customers get great service, it makes your job better in so many ways.

Here are a few tips that will help you better your customer service by taking a walk in your customer's shoes.

Mentally walk through the entire process of customer interaction. It may help to write down the steps or sketch out a flow chart. At every stage, examine how you and/or the company may be coming across. Think about the feedback you frequently hear. For instance, do customers really like the automated phone service or do they seem irritated by the fact that it's so hard to talk to a human being? Is there a problem keeping popular items in stock? Is your return policy confusing or difficult?

If you spot a potential problem, you might be able to figure out a solution you can implement yourself. Most likely, though, you'll need to get the boss or other leaders involved. Remember, especially if you deal directly with customers, you're in the perfect position to know what needs to change.

Just ask customers how you or the organization can better serve them. More importantly, be open to their answers! If a customer says, "Well, Company X does it this way and I like it better," consider whether you can offer that service as well. Again, you may have to go to the boss, but don't hesitate to do so if you think it's warranted.

Look for ways to alleviate customer anxiety. When people are making a purchase (especially when it's a big one) or working with a company for the first time, they feel anxiety. They often don't know what to expect and their minds are racing with questions: *Is this product or service worth the money? How long will the service or transaction take? Later, will I be glad I made the purchase—and will I be glad I chose this organization?*

Anything you can say or do to help the customer feel good about their decision will have a big impact. Whether it's telling them how much you like the product they chose, or telling them you too have had this medical procedure and it was no big deal, or directing them to the endorsement page of your company website, they'll be a lot happier that they chose your organization.

Remind customers about upcoming meetings or appointments. A big part of looking at the world through customers' eyes is realizing that they are just as busy as you are. They're likely to forget upcoming appointments—that is, unless you remind them. Make it a habit of calling or e-mailing customers a few days before an appointment to remind them of the date, time, and other important details. If you're a tax accountant, you might remind the customer what documents they need to bring to the appointment. If you're a carpet cleaner, you might remind them to make sure all pets are out of the house.

Pre-visit phone calls and other reminders not only make sure that the customer shows up for the appointment but also that everything will go as smoothly as possible. And if necessary, after the appointment, make a follow-up call to ask how they liked the service and to remind them of any actions they need to take.

Narrate the service you provide. At every stage explain what you're doing and why you're doing it. Never assume the customer already knows. You work in this field every day so of course *you* are familiar with the process—but you have to assume they've never done it before. Narrating what you're doing will reduce their anxiety and help them appreciate your professionalism.

For example, if you're an exterminator you might say, "My team and I will start by spraying in the doorways and windows. Then, we'll spray in your basement and outside. Don't worry: The chemicals we use aren't harmful to humans or pets. We'll be finished in less than an hour."

Anticipate problems. Make things easy for customers. You probably know where the trouble spots are so be ready to ask, "Do you understand this part of the form?" Also, be ready to provide help (even if the customer didn't ask!). For example, "I'm glad you've found a TV you like. Now let me give you some pointers on how to easily hook it up." If you can help them *before* they have to ask and especially before they encounter the problem on their own, they'll be deeply appreciative.

Look for creative, inexpensive "extras" that make things easier for customers. Here's a good example: An enterprising waiter in an upscale restaurant bought a couple of portable DVD players, complete with earphones, that he made available to customers with small children. He knew that they felt uneasy bringing unpredictable toddlers into a setting where other diners might not approve of their presence. Customers were so appreciative when their child sat quietly through the meal that they lavished the waiter with tips—which paid for the DVD player "investment" many times over.

Take special care to never say anything negative to a customer. (It can't be taken back.) Part of putting yourself in their shoes means understanding why they might get upset or why they might have reacted in the way that they did. Occasionally customers really are being unreasonable, but most of the time they do have a point. (After, they chose your company out of all the others they could have chosen—and they deserve to have their needs met.) And even if you disagree, it just doesn't pay to escalate a customer's irritation or anger—no matter how irritated you might be at the moment.

If you find yourself getting agitated with an upset customer, make an effort to defuse the situation or buy yourself some time so you can get your emotions under control. For instance, you might say, "I understand why you are upset. Trust me, I am going to do everything I can to find out what happened." Acknowledging that you see that the customer is upset and showing you are willing to listen to their problems will help them start to calm down so that you can do the same.

Be aware of your non-verbal cues as well. You don't have to become a body language expert, but it may help to pay attention to how you're coming across. Smile. Maintain eye contact. Don't cross your arms across your chest (this makes you seem defensive and closed off) or let your eyes wander (you'll seem like you're not listening or you'd rather be somewhere else). The idea is to make sure everything about your interaction seems positive and accommodating. You'll be amazed by how well customers respond.

Don't make excuses when things go wrong. You don't like to hear excuses when people let you down, do you? Neither do customers. Just apologize and be ready to make it right. Customers don't want to hear about how busy you've been or how many other customers you've had to serve. Remember, they see things from their point of view, not yours. Acknowledge their frustration and let them know you understand. Then, find a way to make it up to them and always learn from your mistakes.

Nothing matters more than service. The way you treat customers will make or break your organization. In order to make sure you are providing the level of service your customers expect and deserve, it pays to take a walk in their shoes every now and then. When you know where they're coming from, you can serve them better than ever—and the happier they are, the happier you'll be, too.

Chapter Twenty-Seven:

Whenever Possible, Do a Little Bit Extra

What keeps you coming back to your favorite stores, restaurants, physicians, other businesses? In most cases, it isn't their prices or where they are located. It's that the employees at those places treat you well. It's the server who knows your name and exactly how you take your coffee. It's the cashier who gives each of your kids a balloon. It's the store owner who hand-delivers an order to save you the trip to their store. It's the physician who explains the side effects of a medication so you can understand them. You keep going back to places that have gone the extra mile for you, and your own customers won't be any different.

Doing a little bit extra for customers gets powerful results. It can make the difference between a one-time customer and a loyal customer. You end up playing a key role in branding the business as a place that treats its customers better than anyplace else.

The boss will surely notice the great service you provide, and your great service will eventually start to rub off on your coworkers. They'll see how happy your customers are and they'll want to replicate those feelings with other customers.

A story a CEO client once shared with me shows just how impactful going the extra mile can be on customers and coworkers:

The CEO heard that one of his hospital's patient transporters, Steve, had been invited by the family to attend the wake of a former patient. It piqued his interest so much that he asked around and discovered that everyone had an incredible story about Steve. For instance, Steve carried socks with him to put on patients' cold feet as he wheeled them from room to room.

The CEO shared the story at an employee get-together and more Steve stories surfaced. Three weeks later, Steve's father, who lived in a distant city, died. The employees took up a collection and bought Steve a plane ticket so he could be at his father's funeral.

Steve's story not only encouraged his coworkers to imitate his extraordinary level of service, it also built a stronger sense of team so that they all wanted to help him in his time of crisis.

See how it's possible for one person to set off a chain reaction of great service? When you and your coworkers go the extra mile for customers, the company will strengthen its relationships with loyal customers. And having customers you love to serve isn't just great for them; it will very likely boost your job satisfaction as well.

There are many ways to go the extra mile for customers. Below are a few tips that will help you infuse your level of service with the "extra mile" philosophy.

Look for ways to make a positive difference in their lives. Sig Jones was a cashier in the cafeteria at a hospital where I worked. When anyone walked into the cafeteria, Sig's line was the longest. This was not because she was slow at her job, but because people so enjoyed talking with her. She made employees and patients feel good.

Sig knew that some patients were admitted through our ER, and other patients might not have family to help them. She knew those patients would probably leave an inpatient stay in the same clothes they had arrived in. So Sig kept an eye out for those situations. She would take their clothes home with her and wash them and return them the next day. People left our hospital with clean clothes because Sig Jones, the cashier, chose to make a difference.

People like Sig get real joy and fulfillment from serving others. When you serve customers fervently, not only will they be satisfied, you'll be satisfied as well.

Don't always think of service in terms of your job description. Often we stick too closely to serving within the parameters of a job description. It happens for a lot of good reasons—we're too busy to do more than what's required or we're afraid of breaking a rule or stepping on a coworker's toes—but the reality is this attitude can prevent us from providing the best service to our customers.

Sig is a great example. She was a cashier. She didn't work in housekeeping. She wasn't a nurse. But she didn't let any of those factors stop her from keeping an eye on patients' needs and then doing what she could do to fulfill them. Sometimes in order to go the extra mile for a customer you have to step outside the comfort zone of your job description.

Focus on your customers' individual needs. Rather than think of all of your customers as a collective group, think of them as the individuals they are. Pay close attention to the kind of service they prefer and the specific needs they need addressed.

For example, perhaps you work at an auto parts store and one of your customers is restoring an old car. If a part they've been looking for comes in, set it aside for them. The next time they're in the store let them know you thought of them when you saw the part and knew it would perfect for their car. Or heck, give them a call and let them know that it's in stock and that you'll keep it behind the counter for them. The fact that you remembered their specific needs will really impress the customer, and they'll want to keep coming back to a store that provides that kind of personal service.

Throw in unexpected extras. Sure, your customers will appreciate great service, even if it doesn't come with any extras, but when you do provide a little something extra, it gives you a customer satisfaction boost that definitely sets you apart from the rest. There are tons of ways to do this: Have coffee and bagels waiting for a morning appointment. Offer their kids balloons, stickers, or coloring books. These extras wouldn't necessarily make up for mediocre service, but when paired with the great customer service you provide, they'll send customers out the door singing your praises.

Connect before you sell. Your job is to provide great service to your company's customers while also selling them the company's products. Too often while serving a customer we become too focused on the selling side of our job, and forget to acknowledge the fact that we're selling to a fellow human being.

Before you start selling to a customer, connect with them. Ask them how their business is doing. If you know they've recently had a birthday, celebrated the birth of a child, or had some other significant event, acknowledge the occasion. Not only does doing so make for better service, but when you can connect with a customer in this way, they begin to trust you more and their anxiety decreases. They'll be able to have a better experience with the business, and you'll enjoy the customer interaction more.

Always bring solutions. Sometimes your customers come to you knowing exactly what they need, you provide it, and off they go. But when that isn't the case, and a customer looks to you for help or makes a request that you aren't sure you can fulfill, always look for solutions. For example, if a customer needs recommendations for flowers to plant in their yard, you could tell them your favorite plant and leave it at that. Or you could suggest they send pictures of their yard so that you can see exactly what they need. Explain that flowers and other plants can be a big investment and that it's best to do a little research to make sure you get the right plants for the yard. Now that they see your expertise they won't want to get flower advice from anywhere else.

Keep your promises. How many times have you been told by a store clerk, "I'll be sure to let you know when we get that product in," or had a dry cleaner tell you, "Yes, we can absolutely get that stain out," only to find out that neither party lives up to their promise, and even worse, they don't even acknowledge they've failed to deliver? Your customers have very likely had the same experiences. Businesses and their employees make promises to secure a customer's business only to fail to deliver on everything promised. It is the quickest way to lose a customer's trust. Don't ever promise something to a customer that you aren't sure you'll be able to fulfill, even if you have the best of intentions. The flipside is that when you do deliver on your promises your customer will remember. They'll know your company can be trusted to back up what they're selling.

Customers absolutely love it when they feel like they're getting the best possible service. When you go the extra mile, you'll get their love every time. And what's great about going the extra mile is that it doesn't make only your customers feel great. When you see how happy you've made them, you'll be happy too. You'll enjoy your job and it will make coming to work every day truly satisfying.

CHAPTER TWENTY-EIGHT:

VIEW CUSTOMER
COMPLAINTS AS GIFTS

The marketplace provides nearly endless opportunities for customers. If a customer doesn't like the service they get from one company, it's easy enough to move on to the next one. The reality is that many of today's customers don't have the time or the patience to give companies a second chance, and with all the options available, they don't have to.

When faced with an unpleasant experience, many unhappy customers simply leave, say nothing, and never come back again. When this happens not only do you remain unaware of the problems the customer encountered, but you also never have the opportunity to fix them. And that's why it's so important to think of customer complaints as gifts.

Research has shown that it costs five times more to win a new customer than it does to keep an existing customer. Research has also shown that brand loyalty with customers is often stronger when they've had a complaint successfully handled by a company. A good service recovery process is an awesome brand builder. People become more loyal when they come to you with a problem and you show that you can be trusted to solve it. By efficiently handling complaints, you can actually create brand warriors who keep coming back and encourage others to give the company a try.

Know that complaining customers want to give you time to rectify a problem. We often forget that people understand that mistakes happen. When, as a representative of a company, you say, "I'm sorry we made this mistake. Please let us make it right," you now have a chance to strengthen that customer relationship.

When you fix the problem, they learn that they can trust you to provide great service and do the right thing. They see that your service policy isn't just a bunch of words posted at the front of the store or in the employee handbook. It's a living, breathing process that all of the company's employees take seriously.

Read on for a few important factors to keep in mind when thinking about customer complaints:

Use complaints to improve your company. In fact, instead of thinking of them as complaints, think of them as suggestions from customers on what can be done to improve the company. When you receive this kind of feedback from customers and are able to act on it, the company can go from being "good" to "great" in the eyes of the customer. And great companies are the ones customers will go out and recommend to others.

Build greater customer trust through complaints. Knowing that a company can be trusted to correct mistakes or improve on service is a big deal for customers.

To illustrate, let's say you've been using a certain carpet cleaner for a few years. You've been perfectly happy with the service and the company's courteous employees. But after a cleaning, you notice they missed a section of your living room. You call and after a litany of transferred calls and excuses, they eventually agree to come out on Friday at noon, right in the middle of your busy work day, to correct *their* mistake. Well, that's probably not the kind of service you were wanting. It doesn't exactly give you faith that they are dedicated to doing the best job possible for their customers.

What if, instead, the rep had said, "Ma'am (or Sir), I'm very sorry for our mistake. We'd like to send someone out right away to take care of it. When is a convenient time for you? Also, I want you to know how much we appreciate your business. Next time we'll clean your carpet for half off the regular price."

That's a level of service that makes you feel like the company really cares about you. Now, you know that if a mistake is made in the future they'll do whatever they can to fix it. Being able to have that kind of trust in a company is reassuring for customers, and that's why complaints can actually lead to brand loyalty.

Take complaints personally. If a customer comes to you with a complaint, think of it as an opportunity for you to show genuine empathy and personally connect with the customer. You don't have to work in a "helping" profession to want to help others. Just consider how you would want to be treated if you were in the customer's shoes. What reaction would you value? Allow every complaint to send you on a personal mission to handle the issue so well that when all is said and done that customer loves the company. When you view complaints in this way, it makes your job even more rewarding.

Hairstylist Paul Knight exemplifies this attitude. For example, after he cut and colored one customer's hair, he heard that she had told several friends that she didn't like it. Rather than getting upset or defensive, he called the customer up and said, "I hear you're not happy with your hair. Please come back in and let me fix it for you, at no cost to you."

So the customer came back in and Paul worked on her hair until she loved it. Much to his surprise, she posted a big Facebook testimonial about what a great job he had done. Not only was he able to keep the customer, he ended up getting several more—all because he took a complaint personally and turned it into a service recovery success story.

Ask for complaints. Because complaints can play a vital role in helping you improve the company you work for, be proactive. Don't try to avoid hearing customer complaints by hurrying them out the door once a purchase has been made. Instead you might say, "I hope you had a great experience with us today. But if you didn't, we want to hear about it. Feel free to tell me if you have any suggestions, or if you feel more comfortable doing it in writing, please fill out one of our comment cards." Simply providing your customer with an opportunity to voice a complaint or concern reduces their anxiety and helps them think of the company as a place that values their business.

Properly handling customer complaints can make or break a business. With so many options available to today's consumers, the fact that one of your customers lets you know you aren't meeting their needs really *is* a gift. Always treat it as such, and you'll be able to provide them with the kind of service that keeps them coming back.

Chapter Twenty-Nine:

Defusing Unhappy Customers

No matter how conscientious a company may be, sooner or later mistakes will occur. Balls *will* get dropped. Customers *will* get angry, justifiably or not. It's inevitable. In most cases it isn't the actual wrongdoing that makes a customer unhappy; it's the way the situation is handled.

When service recovery situations are handled properly, you have the opportunity to turn an unhappy customer into a customer for life. But when they aren't, you send an unhappy customer out into the world who is *more than* happy to share their bad experience with anyone who will listen. On average, it is believed that an unhappy customer will tell 10 other people. If each of those 10 people pass the story along and then those people pass the story along, it sends out a ripple effect that can be very damaging to a business.

Being able to defuse an unhappy customer is one of the most valuable skills an employee can have. Employees with a sense for great service know how to think on their feet. They know that service recovery starts with "I'm sorry…" and are capable of following that "I'm sorry…" with the right key words and actions. When you provide great service at your organization and can set that example for others, you become invaluable to the boss and the company.

When you've discovered what works, don't shy away from sharing your service recovery best practices with co-workers. If necessary, work with the HR Department to hardwire those best practices for dealing with unhappy customers into the company's policy manual. Those best practices might include the following:

Say, "I'm sorry." I have found that people usually are very forgiving when you simply say, "I am really sorry that happened. What can we do to make it better?" Don't underestimate the importance of those two little key words. *I'm sorry* costs nothing to say…but not saying it can be costlier than you ever dreamed possible.

Sometimes we're reluctant to apologize because we think it means admitting fault. This is a misconception. You *can* be genuinely sorry that someone has been hurt or inconvenienced or that they are deeply upset without taking responsibility for the mistake.

Use AIDET. AIDET is a great way to reduce anxiety ahead of time so that an unhappy customer situation doesn't pop up. It also provides you with guidelines that will help you get back on track if you run into a problem with a customer. We covered this in Chapter 23, but as a reminder, here's how it works:

A—Acknowledge the customer. Say hello and greet the customer by name.

I—Introduce yourself and go over your qualifications.

D—Duration and description of what you're going to do.

E—Explain the important aspects of the service.

T—Thank the customer for their business.

Be prepared with key words. We've all suffered through a bad restaurant experience: You wait an hour to get seated, then you wait another 15 minutes for the server to acknowledge you, then the kitchen gives you broccoli instead of the baked potato you ordered, and then your steak arrives overcooked. In short, everything that can go wrong does go wrong.

At some point during the nightmarish meal, you probably ask to speak to the manager. What happens then will determine whether you return—or whether you boycott it and share the story with 10 of your closest friends. If the manager is prepared with key words, he'll say, "Mr. (or Mrs.) Smith, it seems everything has gone wrong for you tonight. I am so sorry you've had such a bad experience and I want to make it right. I will be taking care of your check tonight and, furthermore, because I want you to return to our restaurant, I'd like to treat you to your next visit. Please accept our sincerest apologies."

Using the right key words is one of the best things you and your coworkers can do to maximize the interactions you have with customers and to repair customer interactions that have gone wrong.

Be open and truthful (even if the customer won't like what they hear). Often, we create problems for ourselves by trying to dodge responsibility or hide problems from customers. If you entered a customer's rush order incorrectly and they're going to receive only 100 brochures for their conference instead of the 500 they need, don't try to blame the printer or avoid the customer's irate phone calls.

Let the customer know that a mistake was made. Acknowledge that you understand that it is going to cause them a huge inconvenience. Then provide a solution and ask what else you can do to correct the situation. Know that this won't necessarily turn an unhappy customer into a happy one, but it will show your customer that you respect them. It will show them that you can be trusted to tell the truth and correct your mistakes. Those are qualities that customers value just as much as flawless service.

Stay calm. When customers are tense or upset, it is very easy for situations to escalate quickly. If you react poorly in these situations—become defensive or disrespect the customer—you've lost their business forever. When dealing with an especially angry customer, stay calm. Don't take anything the customer says personally. Instead, use your key words to speak clearly and calmly to the customer. Eventually your apologetic attitude will start to rub off on the customer. Angry customers usually just want to be heard. They want to know that you know they've been wronged. When you recognize those feelings, their anxiety will subside and they'll start speaking to you more calmly.

Really listen to the customer. Make sure they understand you're taking their words to heart. Upset customers want to be heard. They want concern and empathy from you (both verbal and non-verbal). Do your best to provide it. And really listen to what they have to say. Sometimes customers complain because they want to keep using your products and services and they feel they're giving feedback you can use to improve the company. That's why it is key to show that you are acting on their recommendations.

Frame responses in the positive. In a recent *Wall Street Journal* article about Apple it was revealed that Apple Store employees were encouraged to say, "As it turns out…" when a problem couldn't be solved rather than the less positive sounding, "Unfortunately…"

Sometimes the way you frame your response to an unhappy customer can make a huge difference. For example, let's say a customer is upset because a TV they want to buy based on an ad they saw in the local paper is out of stock. Instead of saying, "Unfortunately, we have already sold out of those," you might instead say, "You sure do know a good deal when you see one! We just sold the last model we had in stock, but I know we'll be getting a shipment in tomorrow. I'll be happy to give you a call when they arrive and will put one on hold for you at the sale price. Or if you'd like, I can show you some of the other TV specials we have going on right now."

Make a note in the customer's file. When a customer has a less than satisfactory experience, even if you are able to correct it, record what happened and what actions were taken. Not only will this help you ensure the same problems don't happen down the road, but it will serve as a great reminder for you to follow up with the customer to make sure they haven't had any additional problems. And if possible, the next time they come in remind them again how sorry you are that they had a bad experience and offer a discount or some other perk.

Follow up with a thank-you note. When you've corrected a problem for a customer, be sure to follow up with a thank-you note that lets them know how much you appreciate their patience and continued business. It might read, "Dear Mr. (or Mrs.) Smith, I wanted to thank you again for giving us the opportunity to correct your order. We truly appreciate your business and certainly hope to see you again soon. As a show of our gratitude for helping us provide better service to all of our customers, please accept this discount on your next order."

One important factor to remember when defusing unhappy customers is that most of them are not after a refund. However, when service has been horrifically bad, I do think it's wise to offer a customer a "financial apology." A full refund, or at the very least a price break or a discount for future patronage, is appropriate. The $50 it costs a restaurant to pick up the tab for a ruined meal is nothing compared with the thousands of dollars it loses when an angry customer refuses to darken its doors ever again and tells their family, friends, and coworkers to do the same.

Remember, an unhappy customer is not a lost customer. In fact, they represent an opportunity to strengthen that relationship and really showcase what a great company you are. When you treat that customer with respect and show that you are willing to do whatever you can to keep their business, they'll trust and respect you in return. That's how you create customers for life. And when you're able to do that for your organization, you become an essential part of the way it does business.

CHAPTER THIRTY:

HOW TO SAY NO TO A CUSTOMER (WITHOUT HARMING THE RELATIONSHIP)

A lways living by the "customer is always right" philosophy can sometimes get you in trouble. There are often situations where the customer *isn't* right. And, unfortunately, the much-used phrase doesn't explain what to do when the customer is clearly in the wrong.

For example, what if a customer requests something that is illegal or completely unreasonable? What if a client wants to make a change mid-project that is going to throw them way off budget? These situations can cause a lot of stress and anxiety for employees, can harm client relationships, and can ultimately damage the company's reputation.

Sometimes saying "no" at the right time and in the right way can help you avoid problems down the road that can cause huge problems for you, the customer, and the company. In fact, when you're able to say no to a customer in a way that preserves and even improves the relationship, you become a great value to that customer and to your company.

The trick is understanding that every "no" has to be paired with an explanation. When you can aptly explain these situations to customers in a way that still makes them feel like they're getting what they want, the boss and the boss's higher-ups will take notice. When you help them understand the *why*, good customers will stay, and those who don't might not have been right for your company in the first place.

Read on for a few lessons in the art of saying no to customers:

If you don't offer what the customer needs, provide an alternative. Sometimes you have to say no to a customer because you simply don't offer the exact product or service they need. But that doesn't mean you have to send them out the door empty handed. You can a) offer a product or service that provides an alternative to what they wanted, or b) recommend a trusted company that does provide what they need.

If you do end up sending the customer elsewhere, manage up that company. Tell the customer about the great service the company provides and let them know that it comes highly recommended. Also, call ahead and let the store manager or employee know you've sent someone over. If you're lucky, they'll manage you up to the customer by saying, "Oh, you must be Ms. Trevor. Jason at Acme Hardware told me you'd be stopping by. He told me exactly what you need."

Remind customers of the agreed upon plan, and why it's important to stick to it. If you're involved with a customer who wants to make a drastic change in the middle of a long-term project, remind them what their original goals were and explain how the change will affect those goals. Perhaps the client wanted to keep the cost of the project below a certain amount or absolutely needs it completed by a certain date. When you point out that the client might be sacrificing these goals, they'll see that you have their best interests in mind, and, in the end, will appreciate that you cared enough to speak up when you saw they might be heading for a problem.

Outline the pros and cons of a customer's request. When a customer makes a request that might not be in their best interests, sometimes you have to level with them. They might not understand the consequences of what they want. Be open and honest about the pros and cons of the request. Maybe your client has been frustrated by a bug problem in their backyard and has asked you, the exterminator, to use your most powerful pesticide.

You might say, "Mr. Lawson, I can use that pesticide, but I don't recommend it. Yes, it will get rid of the bugs and you won't need another treatment for at least a year. However, using it in a small area like this could damage your yard. It is also a strong pesticide so it can be harmful to animals and children." Sometimes that's all you can do. Lay out the pros and cons and let your customer decide.

Pair a "no" with a "yes." Saying no to a customer doesn't mean you have to completely shut her down. There are almost always other options. For example, let's say you're doing some remodeling work on a customer's basement and she wants you to do the electrical wiring in a specific way so that she has outlets in certain places throughout the room. Unfortunately, her suggestions for the electrical would not be up to code and you know you're not going to be able to do it the way she wants.

This is a great opportunity to pair your no with a yes. You might say, "Ms. Arnold, I understand why you would like outlets in these areas around the room. However, wiring the room that way would not be up to code. What if you had outlets in these areas instead? That way they are still convenient, and I can wire the room in a way that is up to code and much safer for you and your family."

Think about what you can do for the customer. Sometimes a customer will make a difficult or unusual request, and it seems easiest just to say no and move on. An example might be if they order something that isn't on the menu or want to schedule an appointment outside of regular office hours. But what if, instead, you didn't focus on what you can't do for the customer and think in terms of what you *can* do.

Think in terms of yes as much as possible. Maybe you do have the ingredients in the kitchen to cook up what the customer has ordered even though it isn't on the menu, or maybe you could come in 30 minutes early to meet with the customer at a time that is convenient for them. Don't just say no to a customer because it is outside the usual parameters. Sometimes by being willing to go the extra mile for a customer you can turn a no into a yes.

Great service means knowing when to say no to a customer, and more importantly, how to say no to a customer. When you can explain why something can't happen and can provide a workable solution, customers won't even feel like they've been told no. In fact, they may be even more satisfied than they would have been had you been able to fulfill their original request. When you're able to say no to customers and still provide excellent service, you'll be invaluable to your boss and to the company.

CHAPTER THIRTY-ONE:

ALWAYS REPRESENT YOUR COMPANY WELL

Years ago, a friend of mine told me that he and his wife had been out for dinner together when they overheard some employees from a local company talking about their employer. He said they were making fun of the company, and sort of bragging about what they, as its employees, got away with.

But my friend didn't tell me this story the day after it happened. He told me two years later when the local newspaper had announced that that company was closing its doors. Now, I'm not saying those employees eating at the restaurant brought the whole company down, but what if all of the company's employees thought so little of it that they didn't mind making fun of it out in public? If all or most of them were going around town saying how they goofed off at work, potential customers probably got the message pretty quickly that they would get better service and better products elsewhere.

Remember, you're just as much an advertisement for your company as a commercial on TV or an ad in the local newspaper. If you don't represent your company well and support the company's brand, why would potential customers want to? When you are out and about in your community you can be a brand warrior for the company. When you proudly wear a shirt with your company's logo on it or tell an acquaintance about a new product or service your company is rolling out, they'll see that you believe in the company. When they see that a company's employees believe in its brand, they'll probably want to check it out for themselves.

Studer Group is lucky to have employees who do a great job of representing the company. They are our best advertisements. A great example of that is a letter we received from a CEO who was visiting Pensacola. His luggage had been lost after a rough day of rerouted flights. At the Delta luggage counter, he said the Delta employee asked, "Are you with Studer Group?" He wrote that he laughed and asked her why she asked. She replied, "Well, I see you are in a suit and are not one of my Grumpies." Then he asked her if the Studer Group folks come by often. She replied, "No, but they always send me something when I help them. I guess they just like good customer service." In his letter, he was kind enough to add, "You do make a great and positive impact and it's not missed by many. Thanks."

Studer Group's employees had represented the company so well that the Delta employee assumed every polite businessperson must be a Studer Group employee. And they had also indicated to the Delta employee through their own actions—by sending a thank-you note or gift—that they know what great customer service looks like. That's what it means to represent your company well.

Here are a few factors to keep in mind as you represent your company, at work and out in the community as well:

Manage up the company whenever you can. Always look for opportunities to sing the company's praises. Now, that doesn't mean you have to talk about the business to every person you encounter, but if you find you're having a conversation where it's appropriate, you might say, "We're doing something really interesting at Acme." Or, "I've been really happy with my decision to work at Acme. They treat their employees just as great as they treat their customers."

We actually talk about our work lives quite a bit. Once you begin thinking about ways you can manage up the company, I think you'll find that you are presented with many opportunities to better the brand by positively representing the company and its practices.

Think in terms of attracting high performers to your company. Naturally, when you talk about how great your company is, or are a great citizen out in the community, you'll attract customers to the company. But you also attract high-performing employees. High performers are naturally drawn to the best. When they hear or read about a company that has a great reputation, they will want to be a part of it. When they see that the company's employees are respected within the community, they will want to be worthy of that same respect.

By being a great employee and singing the company's praises whenever you can, you become a beacon for the company's HR Department and draw in applicants of a high caliber.

Show you're proud to be with the company. Sure, you can talk until you're blue in the face about how much you love to work at a company, and if someone is willing to listen that is absolutely what you should do. But there are also more subtle ways to show that you are proud of where you work. For example, you can wear your pride. When you know you are going to be at a big community event such as a local festival, wear a piece of clothing with your company's name on it or carry a bag with the company's logo on it. Or if your company makes them, put a bumper sticker or magnet with the company's name on your car.

People will see you and think, *Oh, there's Pete. What a nice guy! I didn't know he worked for Acme Products.* They'll associate their good opinion of you with the company. You've worked the company into their subconscious and you haven't even shaken their hand yet.

Prepare an elevator speech. When you're at a neighborhood holiday party, out to dinner with your spouse, or at any other community event, how do you respond when someone asks, "How's work?" Do you give a short, dismissive response like "Oh, it's work. You know how it is"? What if, instead, you had a quick elevator speech that helped you manage up the company and tell, in a positive way, what you've been working on? For example, you might say, "Actually, we just launched this new product, and I think it's going to be really cool. I've helped develop it from the ground up..." or, "You know I've really been proud of how we've weathered this year's economic challenges. The company really stuck by its employees."

It's also great to have an elevator speech about what the company does for when you meet someone for the first time and they ask you what you do. Be sure you can tell them in a quick but clear way what the company does and what you do for the company. For example, "I work at Lake Mills Golf Club. It is a great 18-hole course with a super restaurant." In three sentences, you've managed up the company and its employees. That positivity will really stick with people.

Watch what you say in cyberspace. Be careful not to "vent" about your company on a public forum. For one thing, if you post something negative about your company on Facebook, there's a good chance someone you work with will see it. (Word may or may not get back to the boss, but obviously you don't want to take the chance. You could get fired. Also, you don't want to get a reputation for being a complainer.) But the biggest risk is that a customer or client—or a prospect—will see it. All they have to do is Google your company's name... and in a couple of seconds their image of you could be shattered forever.

Most of us probably already represent our companies well. We speak respectfully of the people we work with and the company's new products or services. We try to look our best when we are out in public and always act as good citizens. But small changes can make a huge difference in the public image you create of the company. Remember, you are a brand ambassador for the company, whether you're on the clock or not. When you strive to always be a great representative of the company you become an even more valuable part of its operations.

A FINAL WORD
FROM QUINT

T hank you to the many who over the years have shared your work, challenges, and solutions with me. Your trusting me made this book possible. I have great respect for the men and women who really make work *work*.

Like some of you, I have experienced the internal pain of being in a job that just is not working. Looking back I have had those "aha" moments in which things crystallized. While grateful I got it, I also wished I could have gotten it sooner. That brings me to my goal with this book. I hope it helps prevent some situations that could be painful, and provides you with a set of tools to make your work better. When we like our work, lots of other things outside of work seem to improve.

I have spent a great deal of time with individuals in administrative/managerial positions. Sure, there are some who should not be in these positions. Still, for the great majority, they are people who each day do their very best work. One does not know how difficult a job role is until they're in it. Thank you for taking on these roles. You have a key impact on those you supervise.

I have found employees take their boss home. The family knows who you are. They know what their spouse or mom or dad thinks of you.

Once when a person introduced me to speak at a large conference he said, "Quint Studer has received lots of awards." My statement when I began my talk was that the best award a person can receive is when people go home and tell their family, "I work for or with a good person." That is the pebble that impacts every drop of water in the pond.

Each person's role is important. Please don't ever underestimate the difference one person can make. That person may very well be you.

I am grateful you took time to read this book. I hope our paths cross someday. Please don't hesitate to go to the Studer Group website at www.studergroup.com or write me direct at quint@studergroup.com.

Thank you.
Quint

ACKNOWLEDGMENTS

T he knowledge and experience of countless leaders and employees at every level went into this book. Their accumulated wisdom shines from every page. I owe these people—the men and women I've worked alongside, coached, observed, and learned from over the past few decades—a debt of gratitude.

Once the first draft of *The Great Employee Handbook* had been written, I opened it up to the feedback of Studer Group partners, coaching staff, and other colleagues. I wanted this book to be the best it could be. I was pleased to see how many of them came back with a wealth of fresh insights, stories, and words of encouragement.

Professionals from some of the top healthcare organizations in the U.S. shared their perspectives:

Wayne Smith, CEO
Community Health Systems
Franklin, TN

Charlotte Burns, CEO
Hardin Medical Center
Savannah, TN

Brian Keeley, President & CEO
Baptist Health South Florida
Coral Gables, FL

Edward Goldberg, President & CEO
St. Alexis Medical Center
Hoffman Estates, IL

Steve Simonin, CEO
Wright Medical Center
Clarion, IA

Jill Grandas, Executive Director
DCI Donor Services
Nashville, TN

Michael T. Harris, MD,
Chief of Surgery and Chief of Surgical Services
Englewood Hospital and Medical Center
Englewood, NJ

Rick Floyd, FACHE, President & CEO
Sherman Hospital
Elgin, IL

Pauline Grant, CEO
North Broward Medical Center
Deerfield Beach, FL

Jack Barto, CEO
New Hanover Regional Medical Center
Wilmington, NC

David S. Fox, President
Advocate Good Samaritan Hospital
Downers Grove, IL

Michael Jellinek, President
Newton Wellesley Hospital
Newton, MA

Dale Knee, CEO
Covenant Hospice
Pensacola, FL

Anthony L. Spezia, FACHE, EHFMA,
President & CEO
Covenant Health
Knoxville, TN

Kerrie Barney, RN, BSN, CHPN,
Director of Project Management
Michigan Center for Clinical Systems Improvement
Grand Haven, MI

Patrick Pianezza, MHA, NREMT-P,
Manager of Service Excellence
San Joaquin Community Hospital
Bakersfield, CA

Kevin A. Sheridan,
Senior Vice President – HR Optimization
Avatar HR Solutions, Inc.
Chicago, IL

Mary Grace Gibson, Respiratory Therapist
EMH Health Care
Bellevue, OH

Andi Coniglio, RN, Director of Surgical Services
Sonora Regional Medical Center
Sonora, CA

Bridget Kelly, Nurse Manager
Hill Haven
Webster, NY

Pat Farrington, Secretary
Porter Hospital, Respiratory Department
Valparaiso, IN

Cathy Phillips, RN, Director of Dialysis
West Georgia Health
La Grange, GA

Jeremiah Kirkland, MSHA, BS, CPS, Administrative
Fellow & External Healthcare Program Director
Rochester General Health System
Rochester, NY

Susan Phelps, RN, MSN, MHA,
Director Emergency Services
Southeastern Regional Medical Center
Lumberton, NC

Kathy Ryan, RN, BS, Service Excellence Manager
Genesis Health System
Davenport, IA

John J. Buckley, FACHE, Chief Administrative Officer
Geisinger Wyoming Valley Medical Center
Wilkes-Barre, PA

Lori Cihon, RN, BSM,
Director of Nursing - Inpatient Services
SouthWest General Health Center
Middleburg Heights, OH

Yvette Million, Manager, Service Excellence
O'Connor Hospital
San Jose, CA

David Callecod, FACHE, President/CEO
Lafayette General Medical Center
Lafayette, LA

Susie Payne, RN, MSHA,
Director of Critical Care Services
Florida Hospital Waterman
Tavares, FL

Anita Zefo, RD, Director, Food and Nutrition Services
Sutter Medical Center
Sacramento, CA

Gerri Buss, MS, RN,
Process Improvement Specialist / Black Belt
Blessing Hospital
Quincy, IL

Lisa Conway, Medical Assistant
East Hill Psychiatric Clinic
Pensacola, FL

Studer Group coaches and other team members
contributed insights as well:

Stephanie Baker, Coach
La Mesa, CA

Kathy Becker, Coach
Easley, SC

Bill Bielenda, Coach
Gulf Breeze, FL

Rich Bluni, Coach
Winter Springs, FL

Tonia Breckenridge, Coach
Nampa, ID

Lara Burnside, Coach
Pensacola, FL

Pam CapoBianco, Coach
McHenry, MD

Debbie Cardello, Coach
Summerfield, FL

Lauren Charles, Coach
Cuyahoga Falls, OH

Donny Cook, Coach
Birmingham, AL

Karen Cook, Coach
Hays, KS

Lynne Cunningham, Coach
Sacramento, CA

Don Dean, Coach
Homer Glen, IL

Lavonne Dwinal, Coach
St. Paul, MN

Jill Ellis, Coach
Stockbridge, GA

Cyndi Fowler, Coach
Kingston, TN

Karen Fraser, Coach
Charleston, SC

Jackie Gaines, Coach
Apex, NC

Cathy Grubbs, Coach
Loganville, GA

Barbara Hotko, Coach
Whitehouse Station, NJ

Judy Kees, Coach
Shelbyville, KY

Jan Knickerbocker, Coach
Fayetteville, NY

Carolyn Laughlin, Coach
Seville, OH

Angela Law, Coach
Pensacola, FL

Jeanne Martin, Coach
Pensacola Beach, FL

Colleen McCrory, Coach
Atlanta, GA

Julie O'Shaughnessy, Coach
Manchester, NH

Greg Paris, Coach
Albia, IA

Lisa Reich, Coach
Aberdeen, SD

Cynthia Schafer, Coach
Aiken, SC

Regina Shupe, Coach
Cincinnati, OH

Joy Skovira, Coach
Hot Springs, VA

Dan Smith, Coach
San Antonio, TX

Deb Strickland, Coach
Murfreesboro, TN

Pat Treiber, Coach
High Bridge, NJ

RaNae Wright, Coach
Mason, OH

Alida Zamboni, Coach
Glen Ellyn, IL

Audrey McDonald, Partner Relations Coordinator

Autumn Morris, Partner Relations Coordinator

Barbara Rouillier, Coach Resource Specialist

Brenda Cantrell, HR Benefits Administrator

Brian Kennedy, IT Support

Brian Porter, Solutions Specialist

Cathy Outzen, HR Administrative Assistant

Charles Cripple, Solutions Support

Daniel Pennington, Media Production Specialist

Debbie Ritchie, Operations Leader

Derrike Nunn, IT Support

Felicia Wynne, Executive Administrative Assistant

George Scarborough, Rural and Studer Covenant Hospice Business Development

Guy Livingston, Data Analyst

Jackie Neese, Executive Administrative Assistant

Jamie Stewart, Publishing Marketing Specialist

Janet Pilcher, Education Leader

Kari Nowak, Finance

Kat Davis, Partner Development Specialist

Kathleen Dean, Accounts Payable

Kelly Dickey, Partner Relations Coordinator

Kelly Ozburn, Partner Relations Coordinator

Kim Bixler, Partner Relations Coordinator

Lauren Hughes Holstman,
Partner Relations Coordinator

Lisa Dailey, Partner Website Specialist

Mallory Studer, Marketing Assistant

Mary Ellen Lott, Research Specialist

Matteo Rebeschini, IT Solutions Implementation Coordinator

Rodney Scott, Finance Leader

Sara Harris, Graphic Designer

Sarah Messer, Finance

Shannon Libbert, HR Leader

Stacy Tompkins, Partner Relations Coordinator

Stephanie Barbee, Meeting Planner

Stephanie Striepeck, Partner Relations Coordinator

Susan Hoover, Solutions Specialist

Tasha Wells, Marketing Coordinator

Tom Northrup, Solutions Specialist

Wayne Hyde, IT

Wendi Ochs, Solutions Project Relations Coordinator

I am grateful to everyone who reviewed the manuscript. You didn't have to do it. That you took time out of your busy lives to make this book better means so much to me.

Thank you to Bekki Kennedy for overseeing the production of this book. She worked to brainstorm chapter topics, narrow them down to the best of the best, and manage a million and one details along the way.

Jamie Stewart, Candace Edwards, Cindy Skipper, Jackie Neese, and Allee Blay helped sort through and organize materials and e-mails sent by all the contributors. It's one of those behind-the-scenes tasks that make a big impact on the final product.

Finally, thank you to DeHart & Company for editing, proofreading, and bringing this book to design.

I loved writing this book. Part of the reason is that I am passionate about the subject. Another is that all of the people listed above—and thousands of others whose paths have crossed mine over the years—made it a fun and energizing process. Thank you all.

RESOURCES TO HELP YOU THRIVE IN THE PAY-FOR-PERFORMANCE ERA

Access additional resources at www.studergroup.com.

ABOUT STUDER GROUP:

Learn more about Studer Group by scanning the QR code with your mobile device or by visiting www.studergroup.com/about_studergroup/index.dot.

Studer Group® helps over 800 healthcare organizations in the U.S. and beyond achieve and sustain exceptional clinical, operational, and financial outcomes. As they face ever greater quality demands—HCAHPS, Core

Measures, preventable readmissions, hospital-acquired conditions, and more—they engage us to help them create cultures of execution. Using our Evidence-Based Leadership℠ framework as the starting point, we hardwire processes that get them aligned, accountable, and agile so they can execute proven tactics quickly, consistently, and in the right sequence…and sustain the results over time. We also help them foster better integration with physicians and other service providers in order to create a smooth continuum of patient-centered care.

STUDER GROUP COACHING:

Learn more about Studer Group coaching by scanning the QR code with your mobile device or by visiting www.studergroup.com/coaching.

Healthcare Organization Coaching

As value-based purchasing changes the healthcare landscape forever, organizations need to execute quickly and consistently, achieve better outcomes across the board, and sustain improvements year after year. Studer Group's team of performance experts has hands-on experience in all aspects of achieving breakthrough results. They provide the strategic thinking, the Evidence-Based Leadership framework, the practical tactics, and the ongoing support to help our partners excel in this high-pressure environment. Our performance experts work with a variety of organizations, from academic medical centers to large healthcare systems to small rural hospitals.

Emergency Department Coaching

With public reporting of data coming in the future, healthcare organizations can no longer accept crowded Emergency Departments and long patient wait times. Our team of ED coach experts will partner with you to implement best practices, proven tools, and tactics using our Evidence-Based Leadership approach to improve results in the Emergency Department that stretch or impact across the entire organization. Key deliverables include improving flow, decreasing staff turnover, increasing employee, physician, and patient satisfaction, decreasing door-to-doctor times, reducing left without being seen rates, increasing upfront cash collections, and increasing patient volumes and revenue.

Physician Integration & Partnership Coaching

Physician integration is critical to an organization's ability to run smoothly and efficiently. Studer Group coaches diagnose how aligned physicians are with your mission and goals, train you on how to effectively provide performance feedback, and help physicians develop the skills they need to prevent burnout. The goal is to help physicians become engaged, enthusiastic partners in the truest sense of the word—which optimizes HCAHPS results and creates a better continuum of high-quality patient care.

BOOKS: categorized by audience

Explore the Fire Starter Publishing website by scanning the QR codes with your mobile device or by visiting www.firestarterpublishing.com.

<u>Senior Leaders & Physicians</u>
Leadership and Medicine—A book that makes sense of the complex challenges of healthcare and offers a wealth of practical advice to future generations, written by Floyd D. Loop, MD, former chief executive of the Cleveland Clinic (1989-2004).

Engaging Physicians: A Manual to Physician Partnership—A tactical and passionate roadmap for physician collaboration to generate organizational high performance, written by Stephen C. Beeson, MD.

Straight A Leadership: Alignment, Action, Accountability—A guide that will help you identify gaps in Alignment, Action, and Accountability, create a plan to fill them, and become a more resourceful, agile, high-performing organization, written by Quint Studer.

Excellence with an Edge: Practicing Medicine in a Competitive Environment—An insightful book that provides practical tools and techniques you need to know to have a solid grasp of the business side of making a living in healthcare, written by Michael T. Harris, MD.

Physicians

Practicing Excellence: A Physician's Manual to Exceptional Health Care—This book, written by Stephen C. Beeson, MD, is a brilliant guide to implementing physician leadership and behaviors that will create a high-performance workplace.

All Leaders

The HCAHPS Handbook: Hardwire Your Hospital for Pay-for-Performance Success—A practical resource filled with actionable tips proven to help hospitals improve patient perception of care. Written by Quint Studer, Brian C. Robinson, and Karen Cook, RN.

Hardwiring Excellence—A *BusinessWeek* bestseller, this book is a road map to creating and sustaining a "Culture of Service and Operational Excellence" that drives bottom-line results. Written by Quint Studer.

Results That Last—A Wall Street Journal bestseller by Quint Studer that teaches leaders in every industry how to apply his tactics and strategies to their own organizations to build a corporate culture that consistently reaches and exceeds its goals.

Hardwiring Flow: Systems and Processes for Seamless Patient Care—Drs. Thom Mayer and Kirk Jensen delve into one of the most critical issues facing healthcare leaders today: patient flow.

Eat That Cookie!: Make Workplace Positivity Pay Off...For Individuals, Teams, and Organizations—Written by Liz Jazwiec, RN, this book is funny, inspiring, relatable, and is packed with realistic, down-to-earth tactics to infuse positivity into your culture.

"I'm Sorry to Hear That..." Real-Life Responses to Patients' 101 Most Common Complaints About Health Care—When you respond to a patient's complaint, you are responding to the patient's sense of helplessness and anxiety. The service recovery scripts offered in this book can help you recover a patient's confidence in you and your organization. Authored by Susan Keane Baker and Leslie Bank.

101 Answers to Questions Leaders Ask—By Quint Studer and Studer Group coaches, offers practical, prescriptive solutions to some of the many questions he's received from healthcare leaders around the country.

Over Our Heads: An Analogy on Healthcare, Good Intentions, and Unforeseen Consequences—This book, written by Rulon F. Stacey, PhD, FACHE, uses a grocery store analogy to illustrate how government intervention leads to economic crisis and eventually, collapse.

Nurse Leaders and Nurses
The Nurse Leader Handbook: The Art and Science of Nurse Leadership—By Studer Group senior nursing and physician

leaders from across the country, is filled with knowledge that provides nurse leaders with a solid foundation for success. It also serves as a reference they can revisit again and again when they have questions or need a quick refresher course in a particular area of the job.

Inspired Nurse and *Inspired Journal*—By Rich Bluni, RN, helps maintain and recapture the inspiration nurses felt at the start of their journey with action-oriented "spiritual stretches" and stories that illuminate those sacred moments we all experience.

Emergency Department Team
Excellence in the Emergency Department—A book by Stephanie Baker, RN, CEN, MBA, is filled with proven, easy-to-implement, step-by-step instructions that will help you move your Emergency Department forward.

INSIGHTS FROM STUDER GROUP EXPERTS:

Access current and archived Insights by scanning the QR code with your mobile device or by visiting www.studergroup.com/thoughts/insights.dot.

Quick, to-the-point articles from founder Quint Studer and other Studer Group experts provide critical information and incisive commentary on hot industry issues.

SOFTWARE SOLUTIONS:

<u>Leader Evaluation Manager™: Results through Focus and Accountability</u>—Organizations need a way to align goals for their leaders, create a sense of urgency around the most important ones, and hold leaders accountable for meeting their targets. Value-based purchasing, which forces you to improve faster and faster, makes this more critical than ever. Studer Group's Leader Evaluation Manager automates the goal setting and performance review process for all leaders, creating an aligned organization where everyone is striving for clear, measurable, weighted goals.

<u>Patient Call Manager: The Clinical Call System</u>SM—This agile, HIPAA-compliant system—designed to streamline the pre-visit and post-visit call process—allows you to provide a strong continuum of patient care and position your organization to greatly decrease preventable readmissions. It enables users to modify questions by patient risk groupings, focus in on key initiatives, and expand as imposed regulations grow.

To learn more, please visit
www.firestarterpublishing.com.

INSTITUTES:

To learn more about and register for upcoming Studer Group institutes, scan the QR code with your mobile device or visit www.studergroup.com/conferences_webinar/upcoming_institutes.dot.

Taking You and Your Organization to the Next Level
At this two-day institute, leaders learn tactics proven to help them quickly move results in the most critical areas: HCAHPS, Core Measures, preventable readmissions, hospital-acquired conditions, and more. They walk away with a clear action plan that yields measurable improvement within 90 days. Even more important, they learn how to implement these tactics in the context of our Evidence-Based Leadership framework so they can execute quickly and consistently and sustain the results over time.

Nuts and Bolts of Operational Excellence in the Emergency Department
Crowded Emergency Departments and long patient wait times are no longer acceptable, especially with public reporting of data in the near future. We can predict with great accuracy when lulls and peak times will be, and we know exactly how to improve flow and provide better quality care. This institute will reveal a few simple,

hard-hitting tactics that solve the most pressing ED problems *and* create better clinical quality and patient perception of care throughout the entire hospital stay.

Practicing Excellence: Engaging Physicians to Execute System Performance
The changes mandated by health reform make it clear: There will surely be some sort of "marriage" between hospitals and physicians. Regardless of what form it takes, we must start laying the groundwork for a rewarding partnership *now*. Learn our comprehensive methodology for getting physicians aligned with, engaged in, and committed to your organization so that everyone is working together to provide the best possible clinical care, improve HCAHPS results, increase patient loyalty, and gain market share.

What's Right in Health Care®
One of the largest healthcare peer-to-peer learning conferences in the nation, What's Right in Health Care brings organizations together to share ideas that have been proven to make healthcare better. Thousands of leaders attend this institute every year to network with their peers, to hear top industry experts speak, and to learn tactical best practices that allow them to accelerate and sustain performance.

For information on Continuing Education Credits, visit www.studergroup.com/cmecredits.

ABOUT THE AUTHOR

 Quint Studer is founder of Studer Group®. A recipient of the 2010 Malcolm Baldrige National Quality Award, the outcomes firm implements evidence-based leadership systems that help organizations attain and sustain outstanding results.

During the course of his 27-year career, Studer has spent countless hours creating, harvesting, and sharing best practices from his company's "national learning lab" of hundreds of organizations. He has worked with thousands of employees at every level across a variety of industries. During this time he has identified and studied the specific skills that make people productive, influential, and efficient—and it's this knowledge that makes up *The Great Employee Handbook*.

Studer is the author of six books. His first title, *Business Week* bestseller *Hardwiring Excellence*, is one of the most widely read books in healthcare. More than 400,000 copies of this groundbreaking book have been sold. His second book, *101 Answers to Questions Leaders Ask*, offers practical, prescriptive solutions to some of the many questions he's received from healthcare leaders around the country. *Results That Last*—written to teach non-healthcare leaders how to apply Studer Group tactics and strategies to their organizations—hit the *Wall Street Journal's* bestseller list of business books and is currently in its seventh printing. *Straight A Leadership* teaches senior leaders how to create organizations that can execute swiftly and well in response to a rapidly shifting external environment. Most recently (before writing *The Great Employee Handbook*), Studer coauthored *The HCAHPS Handbook: Hardwire Your Hospital for Pay-for-Performance Success.*

Inc. magazine named Studer its Master of Business, making him the only healthcare leader to have ever won this award. Twice *Modern Healthcare* has chosen him as one of the 100 Most Powerful People in Healthcare. He is frequently asked to serve as a guest lecturer at institutions of higher learning, to speak to a wide range of audiences across the U.S., and to share his expertise with TV viewers, radio listeners, and magazine and newspaper readers nationwide.

Studer and his wife, Rishy, are residents of Pensacola, Florida. Passionate about giving back to the community, they share their time and resources with local and national non-profit organizations.